LESSONS FROM THE
Felt

Other Books by David Apostolico

Tournament Poker and The Art of War

Machiavellian Poker Strategy

Lessons from the Pro Poker Tour

LYLE STUART
Kensington Publishing Corp.
www.Kensingtonbooks.com

LESSONS FROM THE
Felt

Advanced Strategies and Tactics for No-Limit Hold'em Tournaments

DAVID APOSTOLICO

Lyle Stuart Books are published by

Kensington Publishing Corp.
850 Third Avenue
New York, NY 10022

All Kensington titles, imprints, and distributed lines are available at
special quantity discounts for bulk purchases for sales promotions,
premiums, fund-raising, educational, or institutional use. Special book
excerpts or customized printings can also be created to fit specific needs. For
details, write or phone the office of the Kensington special sales manager:
Kensington Publishing Corp., 850 Third Avenue, New York, NY 10022,
attn: Special Sales Department; phone 1-800-221-2647.

Lyle Stuart is a trademark of Kensington Publishing Corp.

First printing: November 2006

10 9 8 7 6 5 4 3 2 1

Printed in the United States of America
ISBN 0-8184-0701-8

To my beautiful wife and three wonderful boys.
No matter what happens on the felt,
I can't wait to come home to them.

Contents

Foreword
by Matt Lessinger

It's 2006, and poker is everywhere. Everywhere! It's staggering! I can barely turn on the television, turn on the radio, or open a magazine without getting a dose of Texas Hold'em. And everyone is playing it. Whether it's wealthy businessmen in the glitzy Las Vegas casinos, old-timers in their local card clubs, or college kids in front of their computers, everyone has a poker story to tell. Hell, you can't swing a dead cat nowadays without hitting some poor schmuck who just took a *bad beat* and wants you to know all about it.

For those players who need to improve (i.e., all of us), there's tons of poker advice out there, and sometimes it's tough to sift through it all. In my opinion, if you're going to read a book about poker, you should choose an author who has experienced the game from a wide range of perspectives. You need someone who has been where you've been and has felt your pain. You need someone like David Apostolico.

What I like best about David's writing is how easily the pages turn. He does not throw a lot of dry theory at you. Instead, much like my *Book of Bluffs,* he asks you to learn by example, and the broad scope of his examples is quite impressive.

As you'll see from the wide variety of hands he describes, he has played in all sorts of venues, for all *levels* of stakes. He's played in home games, in bars, on his computer, and, of course, in casinos. He's played everything from a freeroll (see p. 18) for $100 to World Series of Poker events with $1 million prize pools.

Regardless of the location or the amount of money at stake, he has managed to turn every game into a personal learning experience. And now in writing *Lessons from the Felt,* he has done an excellent job of passing his knowledge on to you. No matter where you play, or for what stakes, you will find in his experiences something you can identify with.

This book is chock full of lessons, just as the title promises. But if you're going to take one thing away from this book, I hope it comes from the "Two Questions" chapter. Namely, never forget that poker is a game of luck in the short run but skill in the long run. Only losers blame their cards. Winners create opportunities with the cards they're dealt. And by the time you're done reading this book, he'll have you thinking about the many ways to create those opportunities. Do yourself a favor, and pay attention.

♥ ♣ ♦ ♠

Matt Lessinger, a longtime professional poker player, is the author of *The Book of Bluffs: How to Bluff and Win at Poker.* He has written for *Poker Digest* and currently writes for *Card Player* magazine and the *Online Poker News.* You can visit him at *www.mattlessinger.com* to learn more about him.

Acknowledgments

To Richard Ember and the entire Kensington team for their continued support for my projects.

To my agent, Sheree Bykofsky, who as always knows how to play to win.

To Matt Lessinger for his support of this book.

To Kristen Hayes, a long overdue thank you for the awesome cover designs for all of my poker books.

To Phil Laak, for reading an early draft and offering his support.

To Christian Galvin, Derek Scott, and Travis Cabe for sharing some interesting hands.

Trademarks

All terms used in this book that are known, or believed, to be trademarks or service marks have been either capitalized or appropriately noted with a ™ designation. Use of a term in this book (whether designated with a ™ or not) should not be regarded as affecting the validity of any trademark or service mark.

Introduction

This book started out as a follow-up to my previous book *Lessons from the Pro Poker Tour*. *Lessons from the Pro Poker Tour* was largely dedicated to hand analysis from select events played on the Professional Poker Tour®—the first series of tournaments limited to the top professionals in the world. I was fortunate enough to gain an exemption into a couple of the events and both played in and witnessed a number of tremendous nuanced plays that could make or break tournaments but did not necessarily make for great television. This book was originally envisioned as primarily a hand-analysis book composed of hands played at every level of Texas Hold'em tournaments. It became much more than hand analysis, although lessons were still taken from tournaments at every level, as well as additional sources.

Poker is a game of never-ending learning. No matter how much you play, you can still learn a great deal from reading and discussing. So many unique hands and situations are available in poker, and being exposed to as many as possible will help you when you find yourself in a new situation on the felt. More important, though, is learning how to think critically about what is going on at the table so that you can develop your own style of play that will prove most profitable for you.

Being a corporate lawyer for close to twenty years, I have been trained to think critically on a daily basis. When I graduated from law school back in 1988, I went to work as an associate at a Wall Street law firm specializing in mergers and acquisitions. The first week on the job, all the new associates went through a rigorous and extensive training. What I remember most is one senior partner's speech. He told us frankly that our work had to be perfect. Our clients were paying for, and expected, nothing less. We had to dedicate ourselves to that goal no matter what the task. If that meant skipping a few meals, then you skip a few meals. If that meant going without sleep for a couple of nights, then so be it. I would soon find out that he was not exaggerating. There were plenty of all nighters during my time there. We literally made sure every *i* was dotted and *t* was crossed—often working for over forty-eight straight hours.

I wish poker were that easy. As anyone who has played the game can contest, you cannot perfect poker. The goal should be the same, though: to play as perfectly as possible. By setting your goal in such a way, you will minimize your mistakes (although you will still make plenty) and maximize your profits on the way to becoming a winning player. To reach that end, always concentrate on the process and not the results. There is a lot of luck in poker, and you cannot be overly encouraged or discouraged by short-term wins and losses. Instead, take a critical look at your play to make sure you are striving for perfection.

So what is this book about? As I was writing this book, my game was going through a transformation. I had been playing so much that I had started to play by rote and was becoming too mechanical. Because poker is a game of imperfect information, you can never play perfectly. As a goal-oriented person, it is difficult to strive for an unattainable goal. Yet, to be the best player I can be, I still must have the attitude that I am going to do everything in my power to reach perfection.

In my quest for knowledge, this book took on a new direction. It became a potpourri of poker principles (and even some nonpoker principles) that have improved my game, and will, I hope, improve yours. I found myself learning in ways and in places I could not have imagined before—from low-stakes games with novices to game shows on television. I was training myself to look critically at many different situations both inside and outside of poker.

Rest assured, this book still contains a lot of poker and even some hand analysis that's sure to improve your game. More important, I hope that the reader will walk away with the ability to learn to think critically, with an increased awareness of what's going on at the poker table, and with the desire to take that extra step and think seriously about events outside the poker arena and the way they can be applied to poker. (Note: While poker is a gender-neutral game, for simplicity's sake, I have used the masculine third person where I could have just as easily used the feminine. It is meant to be neutral.)

LESSONS FROM THE
Felt

Getting Started

Why play no-limit Texas Hold'em tournaments? You see them on television, they're a lot of fun, it's a great social activity, and everyone seems to be doing it. That may be what attracts many people to the game in the first place. But once players dip their toes into the water, many are hooked by the endless possibilities and strategies involved. No matter how much you play, there is always more to learn. Poker is a game of never-ending learning.

Where tournaments used to be played only by the poker elite in such prestigious events as the World Series of Poker® with buy-ins costing up to $10,000, they now have tournaments for players of all skill levels. In fact, millions of players participate in tournaments every week in venues ranging from the family basement to extravagent Las Vegas casinos. Whether you aspire to be a regular on the pro poker circuit or just want to dominate your local home game, there are many lessons to be learned from the action on the felt.

For those just starting out, let's take a quick review of the structure of a poker tournament. In a poker tournament, every player pays the same entry fee and begins with the same amount of *chips*. Once you are out of chips, you are eliminated from the tournament. (The one exception to this is a *rebuy* tournament, which we will cover in a later chapter—see p. 39.) Play continues until everyone is eliminated but one player. That player ends up with all the chips. The chips in play do not represent actual dollar amounts but only serve as a way to keep score in the tournament. So the winner of the tournament typically does not win all the money, even though he ends up with all the chips. (If you are playing a single-table sit and go tournament—see p. 31—then the winner may take all the prize money, although the chip count will not represent the actual amount of the prize money.)

As a general rule, players finishing in the top ten percentile will be *in the money*. For example, if two hundred people enter a tournament, the final twenty players will each win money. The amount each receives will be weighted heavily toward how high they finish. The twentieth-place finisher will get back not much more than his or her entry fee, while the first-place finisher may end up with as much as a third of the entire pool of money. It's important to study the structure ahead of time so that you can evaluate both your personal goal and your opponents' goals.

Many players will be happy just to make the money. They are not concerned about winning the entire thing. Others are only trying to last as long as possible, that is, if they come in fiftieth place out of two hundred, they will feel a sense of accomplishment. That is the wrong way to approach a tournament. Success in poker is always measured in one way and one way only—by how much money you win. Anybody can play ultra-conservatively and outlast half the field. The problem with that strategy is that you have no chance of winning money. The goal is to win money and not just last as long as possible. That conservative fiftieth place finisher is not better than 150 other opponents are. In fact, he is probably much worse, since he never had a realistic chance of winning anything. It is better to go out early so long as you are playing to win.

There is nothing wrong for beginning players to be satisfied with making the money. That is a realistic goal. Ultimately, however, you should be less concerned about making the money and more concerned about shifting your goal to winning the entire tournament. That is where the real money is. And that is why in this book we are going to concentrate on playing to win.

One of the great aspects of tournament poker is that you know ahead of time exactly how much it will cost you. If it costs you $100 to enter a tournament, then that is your total cost. You cannot lose any more money, and you may end up playing for hours depending on how the tournament is structured. For instance, for your $100 entry fee, you may receive $1000 in chips. These chips are yours to play with until you are eliminated or you have won the tournament. They have no monetary value outside of the tournament. You cannot take them with you. As simple as this concept sounds, it is critical to your understanding of the nature of tournaments.

In a cash game, there is no limit to how much you can lose. Sure, you can try to limit yourself to how much you are willing to lose in a cash game, but the temptation is always there to reach into your pocket or run to the ATM for more money if you run out. In a tournament, once you are out of chips, you are eliminated and are not allowed to buy more chips even if you wanted to.

If you sit down to a cash game, it is up to you to decide how much money you want to bring to the table. In no-limit Texas Hold'em, this can create some real discrepancies in the game. Choosing the right game and knowing how much money to buy in for is a real art form. Since you are playing with real money, your entire stack can be at risk at any time if your opponents have bigger stacks. If you are not comfortable with that concept, you will not play your best. If your opponents are willing to risk that stack at any time, you are at a serious disadvantage. In a tournament, however, each player receives the same amount of chips to start. You do not have to worry about an opponent having deep pockets. In the world of poker, tournaments are the great equalizer.

In tournament poker, you can risk a little bit of money to win a lot. Let's look at the payout structure of a sample tournament. Say that one hundred players enter a $300 entry fee tournament. First place may pay $12,000, while tenth place may pay $600. Let's assume this tournament takes about eight hours to play.

Now let's suppose that instead of playing a tournament with your $300, you decide to sit down and play a cash game. A good gauge of success in a cash game is to win one *bet* per hour. If an average bet in your game were $10, then a solid eight hours of play would net you $80. Of course, if you have a great session, you could win more than that. I think it's safe to say, though, that no matter how great your session is, you won't win $12,000 or anything close to that. That's the value of tournaments. You can win a lot more money by risking the same amount.

The flip side of that is that you have to gamble a little bit. While a good measure of a cash game is winning one bet an hour, that will not cut it in a tournament. Win one bet an hour and you will be *blinded out* quickly.

Since the *blinds* and *antes* increase at regular intervals, the action is forced. You cannot afford to sit back and wait for cards. You have to look for situations and opponents to exploit. You can manage risk in a cash game. In a tournament, you are looking to maximize profits while minimizing risk. You have to be willing to take chances you would not take in a cash game if you are going to advance. In tournaments, there will be times that you will be forced to make moves to avoid elimination. The key to success is to be creative in making some moves before you are forced to make them.

In a cash game, you are playing to win money or not lose money depending on the situation. In a tournament, your only goal is to play to win. A tournament does not end until one person has all the chips. That means that every other player will lose all his chips. Since chips in a tournament only represent value as a way to keep score, there is no incentive to save them for a better situation. Say you sit down to a cash game with $100 and are soon down to your last $20. That $20 is still real money, and there is no need to waste it on an unfavorable situation. You can walk away and pocket the $20. In cash games, it is often prudent to walk away from the table when the environment is not favorable to you.

In a tournament, if you are down to your last few chips, those chips have no value outside of the tournament. You cannot leave the table with them. You do not have the luxury of waiting for the right situation. Rather, you have to use all your cunning and skill to find a way to play those chips. At all times, you are playing to win.

In this book, we will look at various tournament structures and the optimum strategy for each. We will also look at general tournament concepts to very specific hand analysis. While every situation in poker is unique, many of the principles learned can be applied to different situations.

Home Game

The traditional home game has been turned on its head in recent years. Throughout high school, college, law school, and postgraduate, I routinely played in a home game. Back then, everything was dealer's choice, that is, everyone had a turn to deal and could pick which game to play. Every game under the sun would come up, from simple stud to night baseball. Rarely, though, would Texas Hold'em be chosen. It was deemed too boring for most games.

The only common denominator throughout those years was that, even though the stakes were small, everyone played to win. Poker is a game designed to be played for something of monetary value. If there's nothing at stake, it's hard to imagine anyone playing that seriously. Well, I hadn't played a home game in over fifteen years until this past year.

We recently moved into a new-construction neighborhood. One of the great things about a new neighborhood is that nobody knows each other and everyone is willing to have social events to get to know one another. One of the men in the neighborhood decided to organize a biweekly poker night. I had met Robert once before. He was a very friendly guy who absolutely loved watching poker on television. Of course, the only thing shown on television is Texas Hold'em tournaments. When Robert sent out his announcement to the neighborhood inviting all to a night of Texas Hold'em played just for fun, I was happy to go.

It would be a great relaxing way to meet some of the new neighbors. I had never played poker for zero stakes before, but this was meant to be much more of a social event than a poker outing. I figured I could have a few beers and offer pointers to anyone interested in learning. I didn't think that anything remotely resembling real poker would be played. Even so, my expectations still managed to be too high. Six of us convened that first night. Of the six, four had little to no experience. When I mean little to no experience, I'm talking that they had to learn everything from square one. I certainly don't mean this to be disparaging. They were a great group of guys who had other interests besides poker. The fifth player was Robert who had a firm understanding of the game but had never played competitively. His sole experience was limited to simulations on computer games and freerolls on websites. Nonetheless, he did understand how to play. As the host, he was very patient and understanding when teaching the rules to the other players.

It was extremely difficult to play poker that night when every hand was spent answering questions and teaching the four newbies each step of the game. Where I had hoped to offer some pointers, it was really way too premature for that. You can't really teach strategy to someone until that person gets the hang of the game first. It ended up being a fun social night as I tried to put poker to the back of my mind. Still, I couldn't help myself. If I am playing cards, I have to play to win. For the most part, everyone stayed in every hand, only calling but never raising. My strategy was quite simple. I only played strong hands and would raise when I did so. Sure enough, I had built up a sizable chip lead before calling it quits.

Of course, beating five guys getting together for a few beers and friendly cards is nothing to brag about, especially when none of them seemed to have any ambition to win. They were there solely to have a good time and rightfully so. That night only confirmed my belief that poker has to be played for something in order for people to take it seriously.

I missed the next couple of sessions but showed up about a month later. I was somewhat surprised at how the game had changed. Before the game was played like a cash game (with no value); now there was structure. We would be playing a single-table no limit Hold'em tournament. The blinds would increase at regular intervals, and once you were eliminated, it was off to play pool. Now I am not going to sit here and try to tell you that everyone had turned into Doyle Brunson overnight. In fact, the level of play was just about what you would expect from people just learning the game.

Players were still struggling with the rules more than anything else. However, I saw a big fundamental difference from that first time: everyone was playing to win. It was a friendly fun game, but everyone was playing in earnest. I'm not sure if it was the prospect of being the first one eliminated (and having to play pool by yourself) or the pure competitive desire to win that was driving people. But there was no mistaking the fact that everyone was trying to play the best he could.

Now this made things interesting for me. I love the game and I'm always looking for ways to improve. I was curious if I could learn anything to help my game. Still, the game did present a few challenges. Most of the players had *tightened* up considerably from the first time. Players were not just blindly playing every hand. Only one player, Pierre, was intent on playing a lot of hands. If he had any piece of the *flop*, he bet or raised. If he missed the flop completely, he still called down to the end 80 percent of the time.

Now as anybody who's played the game knows, if you play a lot of hands, you are going to win a lot of *pots*. In fact, you can have some fairly significant upside swings. This situation only serves to reinforce the behavior, which is why so many beginning players fall into this trap. Of course, at the end of the day, anyone playing this *loose* is destined to lose all his chips. Watching Pierre play, I thought of what I think is my biggest weakness. When I get a *big stack*, I have a tendency to play too loose. This is something I have known for a while and continue to work on. However, to see Pierre make such a common beginner's mistake was a real eye-opener for me.

When I get a big stack while playing in bigger tournaments, things are obviously going well for me. Yet, I was falling into the same beginner's trap of starting to feed off that positive reinforcement, that is, I'm winning hands, so I should play more of them. Now there are times to play more aggressively with a large stack in a tournament. Yet, I still need to be selectively aggressive and not just craving action.

All right, back to the home game. As sincerely as everyone was playing, nobody except for Robert had anything more than an elementary understanding of the game. I thought it would be easy to pick up *tells* on these guys, but the opposite was true. It is impossible to *put someone on a hand* when he does not know himself what he has. Let me clarify that statement so that it does not sound so disparaging. What I mean is that since these players were just beginning, they did not know the relative strengths of their hands. A player holding any *pair* would stay until the *showdown* believing he may have the best hand. Another player with two pair would be convinced he had a monster even when the *board* contained four clubs and he was holding two red cards. This teaches a valuable lesson. While these guys were playing unintentionally unpredictably, it shows the significance of mixing up your play in order to keep your opponents from getting a read on you.

So the strategy for that first tournament was quite simple: I just laid back and observed for the most part. I would only play medium-strong to strong hands. I played just a few hands, but when I did, I bet them strong and would get paid off. I realized early on that Robert would be the only one who posed any kind of threat. When we were down to three players and I had a sizable chip lead, the following hand came up. I had A♥-Q♥ when the flop came A-10-7 with two spades. Robert led out betting and I re-raised him *all-in*. I did not want him *chasing* a *flush*. Robert called with A♠-5♣. Robert ended up hitting *runner-runner* spades and *doubling up*. Oh well, that's poker.

Soon thereafter the third player was eliminated, and it came down to Robert and me *heads-up*. I had a small chip advantage. Now a funny thing happened. I had been having a good time enjoying everyone's company and feeling very relaxed. All of a sudden, I tightened up. We were playing strictly for fun and pride, but something came over me. I had absolutely nothing to win and a lot to lose. Since I knew something about poker and had a great deal more experience than anyone else, I was expected to win. If I lost, though, I would lose credibility. At least, that's the way I saw it. I'm sure the rest of the group, all being good guys, would not think anything either way.

Well, as soon as you start playing not to lose, you are guaranteed not to win. Robert played very aggressively as you must when you are heads-up and the blinds are high. I played tentatively, waiting for an opportunity to exploit. Instead, I was outplayed and ended up coming in second. Again, I learned a valuable lesson from what I thought would be just a fun social event. No matter what the circumstances, to play not to lose is a poor choice. There will be times in a tournament to tighten up, but to play not to lose anytime is wrong. Unless you are playing a satellite (see p. 42), tournament payouts are always weighted heavily toward the top. If you want to win the big money, you always have to be playing to win.

A perfect example of this is when bubble time approaches in a tournament. Many players are content just to make the money. Others want to win the tournament or at least advance as far as they can. Those who want to make the money will play not to lose at that point in time. The more experienced players will take advantage of this.

Our neighborhood home game continued to be played on a regular basis. It was both fun and interesting to me. It was a great social event, and I learned you could really learn something from every situation. During this time, I was playing in events on the Professional Poker Tour, the World Series of Poker Circuit, and the World Series of Poker itself. I saw players on each of those events making some of the same mistakes as players in my home game. I really looked forward to playing in the home game.

Over the last few years, poker has become somewhat of a job to me. To be able to play purely for fun serves as a reminder of why I love the game so much. That is another lesson learned. Poker should be fun. You have to stay focused and play to win, but you should be having fun doing it. I find that I play better when I am enjoying myself. That does not mean that the game is stress free. Far from it. But it's like any other worthwhile endeavor. I find the challenges exhilarating.

It was fun to watch the different players develop during the course of the home game. I did not believe that any of the guys were playing anywhere else besides the home game. At least if they were, they were not telling. And I could not make every home game with my schedule. Still, I could really witness each player develop and find his own unique style.

First, there was Gib. Shortly after our very first game, my first book *Tournament Poker and The Art of War* was released. Gib was kind enough to come to a signing at a local bookstore and pick up a copy. He also read the book, which showed that he was interested in learning. The fact that he wanted to learn and realized that outside sources could help made a big difference in his game. The next time we played, he was a completely different player. While the other players were making baby steps, Gib made a quantum leap. He was playing very few hands, and when he did, he played them with strength. The two of us easily played the least amount of hands. Not coincidentally, the game came down to the two of us play-ing heads-up. We started with approximately the same amount of chips.

I was not about to make the same mistake again. This time, I played to win and was extremely aggressive. It did not take long for me to win. The biggest mistake Gib made was failing to adjust his starting hand require-ments when we were heads-up. Otherwise, I was extremely impressed with how much Gib had improved in such a short time. He really grasped the concept of using your chips as power, which is so important in a no-limit Hold'em tournament. He did not needlessly squander his chips at any point. You could tell that Gib was also beginning to understand the relative value of hands. He tightened up his starting hand requirements. This paid off in a big way, for when he entered a pot, he was typically a *big* favorite to win.

The two biggest weaknesses I could see in everyone's game was the fail-ure to make adjustments and the failure to use position. Most of the play-ers appeared to play their hands in a vacuum, that is, so long as they liked what they had in their own hand, they played it the same regardless of what else was going on. They failed to adjust to the number of opponents entering the pot, the size of the blinds, the number of players still in the game, and the hands their opponents might be holding. Just as important, they never used position to their advantage. No one adjusted his starting hand requirement even if everyone *folded* to him on the *button*.

Now since these were all beginning players, their failure to make ad-justments is completely understandable and easily excused. Yet, I see it happen all the time in much bigger events. So many things change in tour-nament poker that you constantly have to adapt if you want to succeed. The blinds increase, antes are introduced, players are eliminated, tables are consolidated, and stacks can go from big to small (and vice versa) in one hand. You cannot go into cruise control for one minute. Unlike a cash game, in which you can be playing with the same opponents for hours on end at the same levels (and players can dip into their pockets and replen-ish their stacks if need be), the only constant in a tournament is change.

To make adjustments constantly is very difficult. The consequences of failing to adjust are apparent when watching a table of beginners. The slight adjustments needed to survive and thrive in a more competitive environment are not as apparent but equally destructive to your chances to win. I was determined to work on this aspect of my game after this home-game session.

Let's next take another look at Robert, our host of the home game. Here's a guy with a ten-man poker table, clay composite chips, a card shuffler, dealer button, and every other poker paraphernalia imaginable. The guy loves poker and understands the value of hands. In addition, he knows when to bet and raise. The other guys outside of Gib still prefer to call and *check* just about every time. Robert also loves to *bluff*, and that's his biggest fault at the poker table. He learned it from watching edited final tables on television where they're going to show an inordinate amount of bluffing. A common belief of beginning poker players is that poker is all about bluffing. Certainly, bluffing plays a large part, but it's much smaller than beginning players think.

Texas Hold'em is about playing position and your opponent. It's about making correct decisions and avoiding mistakes. And yes, it's about bluffing at opportune times. Bluffing only works when you try it in the right situation and against the right opponent. In tournaments, the ability to choose spots to bluff is critical because you cannot always afford to wait for cards. Robert, however, bluffed indiscriminately.

There is an old poker saying that "you can't bluff a sucker." What that means is don't bother bluffing a bad player who's going to call with just about anything. Yet, Robert would insist on trying to bluff Pierre. Pierre was going to call no matter what, so what is the point in bluffing. You're only going to lose chips. Robert would try to bluff me, which was a smart thing to do. If I didn't have anything, I would usually fold even when I knew Robert was bluffing. Why would I do that? I was happy to lose a few small pots because I knew Robert would keep trying. Then one of two things would inevitably happen: either I would wait for a strong hand and trap Robert or I would wait for the blinds to increase and then re-raise him when he was bluffing no matter what I had.

We usually played with a very generous structure. We would start with over $5,000 in chips and the blinds would only be $2–$4. So there was plenty of time to be patient. Robert would usually start bluffing right away. There would be times he would get out to a decent chip lead. But as the other players learned to become more patient, Robert would usually be one of the first people eliminated. Now what do I make of this? I think there are a couple of lessons that can be learned here:

First, Robert became interested in the game from watching it on television. His initial understanding of the game gave him an initial advantage over the others. However, he picked up many bad habits that would not serve him well in the end. The highly edited shows are entertaining but also show only the sexy hands that typically include a lot of bluffing. Playing position and stealing blinds does not make great television.

The other guys who regularly played were learning from scratch. They were taking their real-life playing experiences and learning to improve for the next time. In the case of Gib, he was reading outside sources to supplement his learning curve, and it was making a big difference.

The next lesson to be learned is that as poker tournaments have become more popular, you are going to find players at every level who come out of the gate shooting from the hip. Many players, including some top professionals, are very successful employing this strategy, but it is an extremely difficult strategy to pull off. Most players who attempt it fail miserably. They may get off to a fast start, but they inevitably crash and burn. When you encounter one of these players, avoid the temptation to join the party. Rather, stay focused and patient and play your game. Your opportunity will come.

Now to Robert's credit, he improved tremendously over time. He became more patient and looked for opportunities to exploit. If you combine this with Robert's inherent understanding of the need to accumulate chips, Robert has all the tools necessary to become a successful poker player. He'll attack pots when nobody else has a hand. He also knows when to back off when he's beat. The inherent aggressiveness he shows at the poker table is critical to success. Now that he is learning to harness that energy and use it when necessary, his play has become more unpredictable and he's able to not only bluff his way to some pots but win big pots with aggressive plays when he has a strong hand.

Throughout this past year, the players who exercised patience and waited for opportunities would regularly last the longest in the tournament. Even though we started out not playing for anything, everyone played to win. That's the beauty of tournament poker. You can play for pride since you have a clear-cut winner. As time progressed, a small entry fee was initiated with the winner taking all. I don't think it made any difference in the earnestness of the play because I thought everyone was playing seriously before that.

During the course of the home game I played with some hard-core regulars, some others who came and went, and still others who joined later and became regulars. Let's take a closer look at some of the players and see what we can learn from them. I don't believe Vimal had ever missed a poker night in the home game. The first time he joined us was the first time he had ever played poker. He was there to be social and have a good time. The poker was clearly secondary. He took to the game very quickly, however. While he clearly had no idea what he was doing that first night (which would be expected of anyone playing for the first time), he made great strides. You could tell that he really learned from his experiences. The first night, he played every hand. The next time I saw him, he played any hand in which he had a piece of the flop. After a few more sessions, he was laying down hands when he knew he was beat. Vimal became very patient and let the game come to him. He never forced the action. A few more sessions and Vimal was always one of the last men standing. In fact, on two occasions the game came down to Vimal and me heads-up. The first time, Vimal had a substantial chip lead over me. I just played super aggressively and quickly took the lead before winning out. The next time we played, I had an enormous chip lead over him, and he was eliminated within a few hands.

I think that you can learn a few things from Vimal's play: The first being that steady, solid, patient play will take you very far in a tournament. The next being that such play will only take you so far. If you want to win, you have to be selectively aggressive at times and you have to make adjustments for short-handed play. When we were down to three players and even heads-up, Vimal was still waiting for solid cards. You cannot afford to do that. When you are heads-up, you have to be aggressive. With the blinds high and only one opponent, every pot is worth going after. This doesn't mean being reckless. But you can't let your opponent run over you either. It's an entirely different strategy from playing with eight or nine people at the table. Vimal is a quick learner, though. I have no doubt that he will learn from his heads-up experience and be a much tougher opponent in the future. In fact, the last game (which I did not attend), I heard that Vimal won.

We have had a few recent additions to the game, including a friend of a friend who is commonly known as the guy who never folds. More accurately, he should be known as the guy who always calls. He calls any and all bets every hand. He never folds and never bets or raises. Of course, he is guaranteed to lose every time. While he is playing, though, he can wreak havoc. It is impossible to *steal* or *semi-bluff* as long as he is still in the game since he will stay in the hand. The guy who never folds actually poses some real problems. For instance, say I raise in *late position* with A-Q *suited* and get two *callers* including the guy who never folds. The flop comes 2-4-8 *rainbow*. Everyone checks to me. This is usually a great time to bet out and win the pot. That is not going to happen here, though. So what do I do? I bet enough to force the other player out and get "the guy who never folds" heads-up. Then I check it down the rest of the way unless my hand improves. There is no sense betting into danger. Better to wait until I have a hand and then bet away at the guy who never folds.

Now there's another interesting twist to playing with this guy. He's usually out quickly, so you only have a short time to win his chips. What I try to do then is to isolate him pre-flop as much as I can. Again, if I miss the flop, I check it down. If I get a piece, then I value bet depending on the strength of my hand. While you are likely never to find a player as bizarre as the guy who never folds, a valuable lesson can be learned here. In today's environment, there are weak players at every level. That presents some interesting challenges. These weak players are anxious to give away their chips, and the astute player who picks those chips up will be at a real advantage.

So try to identify those players early on, and then choose spots in which to isolate them. The type of player you'll usually find is the *calling station* who'll check call a lot of hands. The difference between the calling station and the guy who never folds is that the calling station will fold on the *river* when he does not make his hand. Isolate these players, build the pot, and then chase them out. Many players like to start out the tournament rather conservatively. That's a solid strategy as you get the feel for the game. Don't wait too long, though, to attack the weak links. They won't last long, so you might as well be the one to take their chips. This is both an offensive and defensive strategy. You're trying to accumulate chips, but you're also trying to keep one of your better opponents from picking up those same chips.

The last lesson to learn from the guy who never folds is that when a player does the same thing every hand, it is impossible to put him on a hand. I am not suggesting that you call every hand, but some uniformity will actually make it more difficult for your opponents to put you on a hand. Let me offer a few examples to illustrate what I am talking about: Say you never *limp in* from late position if everyone has folded to you. If you are going to enter, you will raise three times the amount of the *big blind*. If you then try to *slow play* and limp in with pocket aces in that same situation hoping to get action, you are actually giving away too much information. Your opponents will be suspicious. You are better off raising your normal amount because that will hide your hand better. In another example, say that whenever you raise from *early position* pre-flop, you always bet out post-flop. Now if you flop a *set* and decide to slow play instead of betting out, you are going to send out alarm signals. You are better off doing what you normally would because that would make it more difficult for your opponents to get a read on you.

Poker is a game of seeming contradictions. For instance, there are times to mix up your play in order to be unpredictable and there are times to play consistently. How do you decide which to do? It's going to be all based on experience and your opponents. The more you play, the better feel you will have for what to do. Playing no-limit Hold'em tournaments is an art form. For instance, if you always bet out post-flop when you have raised pre-flop, then try *check-raising* after the flop when you totally miss the flop. Just as this would have sent out alarm signals if you hit a monster, those same alarm systems should be going off depending on your opponent. Knowing the psychology of your opponent and, more important, knowing what you think your opponent thinks of you will guide you in making these kinds of decisions.

All right, back to the home game. Dave C. joined the game about halfway through the first year. The first time he showed up, he played very few hands, and when he did, he played them with strength. He was finally eliminated in about third place. I thought for sure he had some previous experience, but in fact, he said it was the first time he had played. Dave C. really had a natural instinct for determining the relative value of hands and being selectively aggressive. He also asked me a ton of questions, because he was trying to learn whatever he could. I was happy to tutor him as much as possible. The very next game, which I could not make, Dave C. won. The lesson to be learned here is to soak up as much information as possible every time you play and from all outside sources. Don't be afraid to ask questions. (A few months after he started playing and before this book went to print, Dave C. came in fourth place out of over two hundred players at the first annual Poker Author Challenge Tournament at the Trump Taj Mahal in Atlantic City.)

Finally, let's look at my play. After that initial loss to Robert, I won every game I played for the better part of the next year. My strategy was relatively simple. We had a very generous blind structure, so I would be extremely patient and play conservatively. Tournament poker is all about picking spots to win chips and avoiding mistakes. Since the rest of the guys were still relatively inexperienced (although they were making great strides), they would inevitably make mistakes. Once we were down to three people, I would play much more aggressively. Finally, when I was heads-up, I would turn on the heat. A number of different players came in second over the course of that year, yet they would all make the same mistake. They would fail to make adjustments for heads-up play. They would not loosen up their starting hand requirements. After a while they would get tired of me stealing their chips, and they would make the mistake of calling off their chips instead of being the aggressor and raising me.

Well, after about a year, I finally met my match. One of the guys brought his son to the game who played a lot. He clearly knew what he was doing. As I anticipated, the game came down to the two of us heads-up. At that point, I had a chip advantage. However, from the first hand, he was clearly being aggressive. He was raising each hand. This guy was doing what I normally do. I figured I could set him up. The first two hands I had garbage and folded. We were now close to even in chips. The very next hand, he raised me from the small blind. I called with my 7-8 *off-suit*. The flop came 10-7-2 with two clubs. I bet and he raised me. Not to be out-done this time, I re-raised him. To my surprise, he re-raised all-in. I really thought he was on a flush draw, and I was very tempted to call him. I was not ready to risk the entire tournament, though, on a *middle pair*—especially when I was confident I could outplay him. So I folded.

The very next hand, I raised from the small blind with Q♠-10♠. He re-raised all-in. I called. He turned over A-7 off-suit. The flop brought a Queen, but the river brought an ace, and I lost for the second time since the home game had started. I was completely outplayed. I let my opponent take control of the betting. In most tournaments, by the time you are heads-up, the blinds are so high that every pot is worth fighting for. You cannot be at all tentative. I should have fought harder from the beginning. Chip stacks can change quickly. While I am a big believer in avoiding mistakes during the course of a tournament, at the end when the stakes are high, I would rather err on the side of being aggressive than cautious.

The main reason I lost, though, is that I again played not to lose when we were heads-up. If you're not playing to win, you are not going to win. This actually leads me to the most important lesson I learned from the home game. Every time I went to the game, my entire focus was not on if I was going to win, but how I was going to win. I never doubted that I was going to win. There were times that I was extremely short stacked, and it never even occurred to me that I would not win.

Whenever I play, no matter what the competition, I always expect to win and hopefully play to win. However, until I played in the home game, I realized that I do not always know that I am going to win when I play against tough competition. And that is the attitude that you have to have if you are going to win. Confidence is a tremendous part of poker. If you talk to just about any top professional poker players, they will tell you (if they are being honest) about how they had to work their way up the ranks, that is, they would start out playing a low-stakes game until they could dominate it. Once they could, they would take a shot at a higher stake game. If they ran into trouble, they would step down to the lower stakes and regain their confidence and bankroll.

Every poker player is going to go through a rough patch. Unfortunately, losing is part of poker. When you are going through one of those spells, find a game that you are likely to dominate to get your confidence back. Play some low entry fee sit and go's where the competition is fairly weak. Play them until you absolutely know you are going to win, and then take that same attitude with you to your next bigger event.

Freerolls

Remember when I said that I was amazed that a home-game poker tournament could be played in utmost seriousness with nothing at stake. Having a clear-cut winner makes the game competitive. People can play for pride just like they would if they were playing a pickup basketball game. That same logic does not follow to a big freeroll (a tournament that offers prizes or cash but is free for players to enter), sad to say. The problem with a freeroll offered by an online site or local bar is that none of the players know each other. No one has any desire to play for pride anonymously. It just doesn't work.

So why play freerolls? If you are just starting out, the online freerolls are a great way to get used to the structure and feel of a tournament. As far as strategy, you are going to have a hard time learning anything because these tournaments will be played fast and loose with a devil-may-care attitude. The exception is if a decent prize is offered. There are a number of bar/restaurants near me that offer weekly free tournaments, but they offer first-place prizes up to $200. This changes the game quite a bit. I have done some investigative research and have found the quality of play at these tournaments to vary greatly. While a majority of players are fairly poor, I did find that just about everyone was playing to win.

This situation is quite different from an online freeroll tournament where it does not appear that anyone is playing to win. Many online sites will offer small-fee buy-ins for as little as $2 or $3. As miniscule as that number may sound, it changes the philosophy dramatically. The great majority of players takes the game seriously or else they wouldn't be playing.

Requiring them to pay something, no matter how small, out of their own pocket makes a world of difference. I played a few of these tournaments when I was testing software on the various sites, and they were quite entertaining and competitive. If you want to test the waters online, try a few.

Barroom Poker

The exploding popularity of no-limit Hold'em tournaments continues to amaze me. Within a five-minute drive from my house (located outside of Philadelphia), at least a dozen restaurants/bars hold weekly tournaments. These tournaments are freerolls offering a variety of prizes. Twenty years ago, this would have been nirvana for me. Now the idea of playing in a smoky bar with a bunch of drunks for the chance to win a gift certificate or T-shirt has zero appeal to me.

One of my neighbors who is just starting out in poker has been playing some of these tournaments on a regular basis, so I decided to meet up with him one night to see first hand just how bad or worthwhile these tournaments were. We went to a restaurant about a mile from our neighborhood that has a weekly Wednesday-night tournament. Registration is at 7 P.M. and fills up quickly. So we met there at 6:30 to make sure we got in. Sure enough by 6:45 a line had already formed. The tournament was limited to seventy players, and by 7:15 there was already an alternate list. I was impressed with the enthusiasm. Since the tournament would not start until 8:00, we got a bite to eat. Obviously, the reason places like this hold these tournaments is to bring in eating and paying customers, for which I was happy to oblige.

I was also surprised to find out that there would be a first-place cash prize of $200. Second place would get a T-shirt, and that would be the extent of the prizes. Each player would start with $2,000 in chips with blinds at $25-$50 and levels at 30 minutes each. This seemed like a fairly decent structure for a freeroll. There were seven tables with poker tops on them, and each one had composite chips and new cards. We had two decks per table and you dealt your own. So far, I was impressed. From a purely economical point of view, it would still not make any sense for me to play. Even if I was to win, $200 for an entire night of poker was not a good use of my time. Plus, no matter how bad the play was, there are no guarantees in poker. Even a blind squirrel will occasionally find the nuts. However, I was here to have a good time and to see how good or bad the play would be. I was half expecting the worst and half hoping for some good play.

I found my table and sat down a few minutes before 8:00. One lady had already been there for quite some time stacking, counting, and re-stacking her chips. Maybe she was a *ringer*. Soon, everyone else sat down, and right at eight o'clock sharp, the cards were in the air. The first hand just about everyone limped in loose and passive. I had Q-J suited in late position and decided to limp in as well until I could get a real feel for the game. The flop came 5♦-7♦-9♦. One player bet out $100 and there were two callers. I folded. The turn brought a *blank*, and again the same player bet out (this time $200), and there were two more callers. The river brought the 10 of diamonds and the same original player bet out. This time he bet $500. One player folded and the lady who first sat down called. The first player proudly turned over his J-8 (neither was a diamond) for a *straight* and began to scoop the pot. The lady turned over the 6-8 for a *straight flush*. She had flopped the stone-cold *nuts*. However, it appeared that she had no idea whether she had won or lost the hand. (So much for her being a ringer.) A couple of players quickly pointed out that she had a flush. I pointed out that she actually had a straight flush. Everyone looked at me as if I had two heads and then looked back at the board. After what seemed like a few minutes, this obnoxious guy at the table pointed out (in a manner that was meant to convey that he would be the final voice on all matters at this table) that the lady did indeed have a straight flush. I could tell that this was going to be a long night.

Since it appeared that there were quite a few regulars at the table, I decided to keep a low profile and not intercede unless absolutely necessary. It soon became apparent that I had entered some sort of alternative poker universe. Players were calling off their chips with low pair or ace high. And this was on the river! Everyone seemed to be having an extremely difficult time reading the board. After a showdown, more often than not, I had to explain who won the hand and why. For instance, one player could not understand why his pocket sixes were no good with a final board of Q-Q-8-10-10. He was convinced his hand was better than his opponent's A-4.

You see, since there were two pair on the board, he only had a six kicker to his opponent's ace.

My plan for keeping a low profile was becoming more and more difficult. I had to choose what to correct. I chose to ignore string bets and raises below the minimum. However, I had to introduce the concept of a side pot. Apparently, they had been playing that a short stacked player who was all-in was eligible for the entire pot. On the other hand, I chose to ignore the obnoxious player's habit of shorting the pot. If it was $200 to him, he would somehow manage to put in only $100. I could not ignore, however, his attempt to cheat me.

For the most part, I played tight because I was more interested in observing. In addition, whenever I had a hand, I was sure to get plenty of action. Well, after a few hours of play, the lady without a clue and Mr. Obnoxious were the clear chip leaders at the table. Mr. Obnoxious was winning due to his cheating ways, and the lady without a clue was calling down every other hand and winning most of them. It was impossible to put her on a hand since she herself had no idea what she had. The only time she knew what she had was when she had a set of tens against my straight. Of course, she thought her set was good—which set off a few minutes of discussion before Mr. Obnoxious in his infinite wisdom "declared" me the winner.

Then the following hand came up. I was in the big blind and Mr. Obnoxious was in the small blind. The lady without a clue and Mr. Obnoxious called, I checked my blind, and we saw a flop three handed. I had 5-6, and the flop came 4-8-J rainbow, giving me a *gutshot* straight draw. Mr. Obnoxious checked, I checked, and the lady without a clue checked. Then Mr. Obnoxious bet. Huh? That's right. He bet once he knew that we were both going to check. Of course, I objected, but he insisted that he had never checked. So I folded, the lady without a clue called, and wouldn't you know it, the 7 rolled off the turn that would've completed my gutshot. Mr. Obnoxious continued to bet heavily, and the lady without a clue continued to call. I would've won a huge pot. Even though I was there to observe, my competitive juices took over at that point. It was on. I took off my journalist hat and put on my poker hat.

Either Mr. Obnoxious was gone or I was gone. Since I had position on him, I waited for my next playable hand. A short while later, he open raised for about five times the big blind. I found A-K and raised enough, I hoped, to isolate him and keep him in the pot. Well, the player behind me re-raised all-in. Mr. Obnoxious called and shorted the pot. I called as well, but this time I pointed out Mr. Obnoxious's shortcomings. He got real snotty, but fortunately the other player saw it as well. I stayed calm, and just said, "Let's count the pot and see." Apparently, this was something that had never occurred to Mr. Obnoxious because he quickly became twitchy and decided on his own that he had put in the wrong color chip by mistake.

Just as I hoped, Mr. Obnoxious turned over K-8 off-suit, although the other player had *pocket rockets* (poker slang for two aces). I was drawing extremely thin and never improved. I was happy to give my chips to the other player, though. And as a special parting gift, I informed the table that Mr. Obnoxious had been shorting the pot all night.

Lessons Learned

It's never a good idea to take anything personally at the poker table. Stay emotionally detached. This was a freeroll, and I was there for fun and observation. But still, I had not decided to start playing serious poker until I was already steamed. No matter what the setting, if you are going to play, you should play to win. Bad habits can form from the most innocent of sources. You play for fun one day, and then the next time you are playing seriously, you find yourself playing way too many fun hands.

The biggest lesson I learned from this excursion is that it is not my job to police the table. While I tried to show a lot of restraint here, I could not help myself from correcting a lot of mistakes even when I was not involved in the action. Granted, the players' understanding in this instance was particularly horrendous. However, I realized that my personality type is to want to arbitrate and get involved over disputes when I feel strongly that one party is being wronged. I never really thought that there was anything wrong with doing that.

The problem is that playing referee can be a big distraction. My job at the poker table is to be as focused as possible. I want to observe everyone as much as I possibly can. If I am part of the action, I cannot be focusing. Disputes do come up at the poker table quite frequently. Many players wear their emotions on their sleeves and tempers can sometimes flare. If I get involved, I cannot be observing these players at this critical time. More important, though, is that I run a huge risk of upsetting my emotional even keel.

It's hard enough to maintain composure and discipline over a long period when the cards can wreak havoc on your game. Why make things harder by raising your blood pressure needlessly? Even if I am trying to maintain order by interceding, someone is bound to get upset and direct his anger toward me. I don't need that extra stress. If people want to fight, let them. It's up to the dealer and the floor manager to resolve the problem. Unless I am directly involved, I don't get involved. I save my energy and maintain my focus on the players. If I am involved, I stay calm and make my case to the dealer. If need be, I call the floor manager or tournament director over. I avoid engaging my opponent as much as possible.

Players will often try to get others involved. At a recent tournament at the Trump Classic, two players saw the hand all the way to the river. Player One checked and then believing that Player Two checked as well, Player One turned over his hand. Player Two immediately said that he still hadn't acted. Player One then turned his cards back over and got really upset accusing Player Two of angle shooting in order to see his cards. Player One showed a hand of K-J with a board of 9-J-2-J-6. Player Two then made a huge bet. Player One called without hesitation. Player Two turned over J-10, and Player One won a big pot. Player One continued to berate Player Two and asked everyone at the table to back him up. I didn't say a word, even though I knew that Player Two had never checked. Player One even went as far as to hit the player next to him on the arm and said "You saw it, right?" If this happens to you, the best thing is just to say that you weren't paying attention.

College Night

Not to be deterred, I thought I would venture out and check out another bar/restaurant poker night. This one attracted a younger crowd of mostly college-age people. The event offered one first-place prize of a $100 gift certificate to the hosting restaurant. We started with about fifty people, and I could tell immediately that the level of play was much better. At least most players had a decent understanding of the fundamentals of the game. The biggest mistakes were still made by players betting or raising less than the minimum. I largely ignored these mistakes. The only time I did intervene was when one player did not understand how he could lose a pot holding pocket fours when the board showed 10-10-8-8-2. His opponent had an ace. I'm still not sure that this guy understood that he had two pair (tens and eights) with a four *kicker*. But there were enough people at the table who did understand, so our player with pocket fours reluctantly gave up the pot.

I spent most of the night keeping quiet and studying the other players. Most of the college-age crowd could easily be typecast into typical cliques—the jock, the bookworm, the partier, and so on. At that age, I think many people not only live up to their reputations but relish them. What was interesting, though, is that I found no correlation between stereotype and playing style. Every player seemed to have his own unique style. Some of the jocks liked to bluff and others were calling stations. The same situation was true with the other stereotypes.

While I pride myself on being able to read people, this got me to thinking whether I am quick to make judgments of my opponents even if they don't fit into a neat stereotype. It's almost impossible not to come to some sort of judgment based on how someone is dressed or how he talks and walks. If nothing else, this night served as a reminder to me not to judge a player by his appearance. I want to make sure I am making sound judgments based on playing habits and my thorough read of an opponent's unique personality.

How did the night end up? I went out at the final table when I pushed all-in with pocket Jacks. I was called by A-10 and an ace came on the flop.

Playing Online

The Internet, the last frontier of poker, also serves as the first introduction to the game for many players. Playing online is a great way to gain a lot of experience in a hurry. No commuting time and no hassles, and you can log onto a tournament at any time, day or night. The speed with which the hands are dealt allows you to play at a much quicker pace than in a traditional brick-and-mortar card room. That's just the beginning. There are a number of other distinctive characteristics of online tournaments that are worth discussing.

Sit and Go

Most online sites have some version of the sit and go tournaments. These tournaments run around the clock and range from heads-up play to three-table tournaments. By far, the most popular are the single-table no-limit Hold'em tournaments. As soon as ten people sign up, it's time to shuffle up and deal. These tournaments are offered at various entry fees. With the lower entry fees, the tables fill up constantly, and you can be playing within seconds of logging on.

I highly recommend these single-table tournaments no matter what your level of skill. They're usually over within an hour and rarely go beyond ninety minutes. During that time, you get to play a condensed version of a bigger event with all the same skills necessary to win and advance. If you are just starting out, it's a great way to learn about balancing chip accumulation with survival. In my first book, *Tournament Poker and The Art of War*, I discussed at length the need to strike the proper balance in order to thrive in no-limit Hold'em tournaments.

I see many beginning players make the mistake of being overly aggressive early in a tournament when the stakes are low. This player usually gets off to a fast start, but is easily trapped later on and then ends up being one of the first players eliminated. In single-table sit and go's, this mistake is magnified. Let me explain why.

In a big tournament, say where there are over three hundred entries, typically only those players finishing in the top 5–10 percent of the field will be in the money. And among those winners, the prize money is weighed heavily toward the top finishers. The first-place finisher may end up with 30 percent of the overall prize pool. With that kind of structure, there is a lot of incentive to take some chances at accumulating chips because for many players the goal is to finish number one.

Now let's look at the payout structure for a single-table online sit and go. With ten players, the top three places will win. That's 30 percent of the field! Typically, first place will win 50 percent of the prize money, second place will take 30 percent, and third place will win the remaining 20 percent. Think about it. If you finish in second place, you're only in the top 20 percent of the field. In a multitable event, a top 20 percent finish will win you absolutely nothing. Yet, here you're winning 30 percent of the prize pool, which is the same as the first-place winner in our three-hundred-person field.

How should this affect your strategy? You should be very patient since there's a nice payout for outlasting and surviving into the top third. I find most players do the opposite. For some reason, they think that they have to be aggressive from the get-go. Now the blinds will typically increase every ten minutes, so you can't afford to wait too long. I think you'll find, though, that if you remain patient enough, other players will force the action and make mistakes allowing you to capitalize on them. Then as players are eliminated, I think it's time to become more aggressive. Again, you'll find a lot of players doing the opposite. With only four or five players remaining, its bubble time and many players tighten up. The blinds have usually increased significantly by this point, so now is the time to take advantage of your opponents' timidity to rack up some chips. Once you are down to three players and everyone is in the money, the action will pick up again. By now, you should've been paying close enough attention and have a decent read on your opponents. Play position, be selectively aggressive, and implement typical short-handed strategy.

Another interesting phenomenon I find in these single-table sit and go's is a lack of understanding of the value of chips. I think that there are two reasons for this: First, clicking on your mouse is a whole lot different from picking up hard, cold chips and committing them to the pot. Next, the fact that a player can be playing a new tournament within seconds of being eliminated from the one he's playing lessens the importance for him. Again, you'll see players force the action. It's almost as if they are playing a rebuy tournament. If they get short stacked, they push in their chips and figure either they will double up or they will start a new tournament with a full stack. Keep this in mind and use it to your advantage. Just try to play mistake-free poker in the early stages and exploit the mistakes of others.

By the same token, don't fall into the trap of throwing your chips away when you get short stacked. I can think of two recent sit and go's in which I was down to almost nothing and came back to win it all. In the first one, I was literally down to one $25 chip in the early stages of a ten-person field. The starting stack was $1,500. I was all-in with A-A pre-flop against Q-Q and ended up losing when a Queen hit the flop. I had my opponent *covered* by $25, so I was left with one chip and came back to win. In a small field, even a few chips can make a difference.

In another tournament, an opponent made a big mistake. In the early stages of a six-person sit and go, I raised from early position with K-Q suited. The blinds were $25–$50, and I made it $150 to go leaving myself with $300 in chips. A player in late position who had been playing fairly tight re-raised another $205. If I called, I would be left with $95. Now I think this player made a big mistake. He should have raised enough to put me all-in. So I called. I think many players here would re-raise all-in figuring that they are pot committed anyway. I think that's a big mistake. If an opponent is sloppy enough to leave you with an out, take it. I was glad I did because the flop came A-5-2 with none of my suit. I check folded. A few hands later I pushed in with Q-J suited and got four callers. When I made a *full house*, I quadrupled up and was well on my way to victory.

Finally, another great reason to play sit and go's is that they offer you the opportunity to play short handed and heads-up. If you enter a three-hundred-plus person event, you're going to have to make the final table in order to get that experience. Adjusting to short-handed and heads-up play is a critical part of final table experience. Every time you enter a sit and go, you're playing a final table.

Turbo Sit and Go's

Many poker sites offer accelerated single-table tournaments. On Poker Stars.com, these are called Turbo tournaments. Other sites have similar names. In a Turbo tournament, the blinds increase every few minutes. Certainly, this is a big factor to consider. You are going to have to move fast. Be disciplined but be ready to make moves.

When I first started playing tournaments, I used to make the common beginner's mistake of playing too conservatively. I would get blinded out before making a move. In no-limit play that is inexcusable. Before you lose the power of your chips, you have to use them while they still have some force. If you struggle with this aspect of your game, turbo sit and go's are great practice. Since the blinds move quickly, you must be aggressive or you will be blinded out. Play a few of these in a row. Soon you will be more comfortable making big bets with less than stellar holdings. Just remember that when you go back to a more even paced tournament, you will not need to move so fast.

Heads-up Play

I would highly recommend that any aspiring tournament player play some heads-up matches. First, if you are ever going to win a big tournament, you are going to have to go head to head with another opponent. Adjusting to heads-up play is so important because almost any hand is playable. The game becomes one of reading your opponent and being aggressive. Of course, these traits are great for any poker you are going to play.

Next, when you play heads-up, you will get a good grasp of how tough it is to make a hand. It is hard to hit the flop, let alone top pair or better hands. You really have to learn how to play post-flop without a hand. You do this by using guts and position. Play enough heads-up and soon you will be able to play with guts and use position in any poker setting.

So often in full tournaments, you will be seeing a flop heads-up with another player. There is a tendency for beginning players to abandon a hand too quickly when they miss the flop. They often give their opponents too much credit for a hand in those situations. If you are going to succeed in tournaments, you are going to have to learn to win pots after the flop. In the later stages of a tournament, the pots are just too valuable to give up without a fight. Playing heads-up matches is an excellent way to gain the experience that you need.

Online Tips

Playing online offers the convenience of being able to sit in the comfort of your home and plug into a game any time of day or night. The flip side is that the amenities of home can prove distracting. It's very tempting to try to multitask when playing online. Turn the television on and play some poker. Write bills and play poker. Balance your checkbook, play with the kids, talk on the phone, and play poker.

When you walk into a brick-and-mortar poker room, it's a lot easier to remember to put on your game face. You have to take money out of your wallet and physically buy chips. You get to squeeze the cards in your hand. You have real live opponents to study and analyze. It's easy to see how your total focus and concentration is required in order to succeed. In addition, you have to be in the right frame of mind. Again, this is made much easier when you are face to face with nine other players trying to take your money.

If you're playing poker, you should be playing to win no matter where you're playing or whom you're playing against. Playing online requires the same focus, concentration, and determination as playing live. Don't log in if you aren't prepared to focus 100 percent of your energy to the task at hand. Those virtual chips are worth just as much as the clay composite ones you can hold at your local card room. Don't ever forget that. Online players tend to play much looser since it's a whole lot easier to click on a mouse and throw chips in than to physically pick them up and contribute them to the pot.

Online players tend to be more brazen. They will bluff more since they are hiding behind the Internet shield of anonymity. Many players are embarrassed to get caught bluffing in a live poker game. When to bluff or not to bluff should not depend on your tolerance for being caught. Bluffing is a great tool if used sparingly and judiciously. It will not always work, and there will be times you get caught. So what? So long as it was the right decision at the time, that is all that matters. However, do be aware that there will be some more bluffing online.

So how do you read your opponents online? Certainly, there is no substitute for live play. However, there are a number of things about online play that are the same as live play and even some advantages from playing online that can help you read your opponents. First and foremost, stay focused. Pay attention to the action even when you are not in a hand. Track betting patterns. Take notes. Most sites will allow you to keep notes right on the site. Even better is to keep a big notebook of detailed observations about your opponents. Even though virtually tens of thousands of players are online at any time, if you play the same daily or weekly tournament, you will be surprised at how many opponents you will recognize.

Next, track your own play. Most sites will give you instant feedback for your current session. It will tell you how many flops you have seen, how many hands you have seen to the river, and what percentage of those hands you have won. It is a quick barometer of how loose or tight you are playing. I think you will be surprised at times at how different your perspective may be from reality. I know there are times that I think I am playing well but just think the cards are not cooperating. Then I click on an icon and see that I have played close to 40 percent of the hands, which is way too high. It can be very enlightening and help your game tremendously.

Another aspect of online play is the ability to request hand histories. In a brick-and-mortar casino, if a player stays until a showdown, anyone else at the table can request to see his hand. The common etiquette, however, is not to ask. If a player chooses to *muck* his losing hand, rarely will anyone ask to see it. I would recommend that you stick to etiquette in a live game. After all, if you ask, others will ask to see your hand.

When playing online, each player has his own option of whether to muck or show his losing hand. That is not the end of the story, though. If you request a hand history, you will get to see the cards that player mucked. This is true so long as you are seated at the table even if you were not involved in a hand. Furthermore, the other players will have no idea that you requested the hand history. This information is e-mailed to you instantly. Thus, you could watch a hand played at your table and find yourself very curious as to what the losing player had. You can request the hand history, check your e-mail, and have your answer by the time the next hand is complete. This can be extremely valuable information.

If you do have trouble making moves or bluffing without getting caught, then playing online is a great place to practice. Don't get carried away, but try different things to see how effective they can be. Once you see what works and what doesn't, you'll have the confidence to try those moves at your next live game. The goal should always be to improve, and you should be playing to win.

Brick-and-Mortar Single-Table Sit and Go's

Within the past year, this type of tournament may be the single biggest growth area in poker. These tournaments are now generally available all day at most big card rooms. For tournament junkies like me, they have become more of a staple than cash games. If I have time to kill before a tournament or if I am knocked out of a tournament, these are a great alternative now to a cash game.

Single-table sit and go's are also great practice for a bigger multitable event. They are a condensed version of multitable events and the strategy is extremely similar. The biggest difference between brick-and-mortar sit and go's and the online version is that typically the brick and mortar are winner take all, that is, first place wins the entire pot at a ten-person table. If you recall, online sit and go's typically split the pot between the top three finishers.

So when playing a brick-and-mortar sit and go, you are playing to win the whole thing. Just like in a multitable event, you need to be patient at first, but then at some point you have to adjust and be aggressive. While your game should never be too predictable, I have enjoyed great success by following this basic formula: I start out tight and get a feel for the other players. I study them each individually and pick up as much information as I can. As the blinds increase, I become more aggressive and pick up pots by capitalizing on my conservative image. Then, when we are down to three or less players, I become even more aggressive. I really turn the heat on my opponents and put the pressure on them.

Just like a bigger event, the game gradually switches from a post-flop strategy to a pre-flop one as the blinds increase and players are eliminated. By the time I am heads-up, I am going to push any edge pre-flop.

I find that many players do not adjust their starting hand requirements nearly as much as they should as the field thins. A lot more hands are playable three handed than would be ten handed or even six handed. When the players finally get sick of being pushed around, they are likely to make a big mistake. Let me offer some examples.

If I feel a slight edge, I am going to push it when we are down to three or less players. Hands such as K-10, Q-J, J-9, or any ace are hands that I am going to push extremely hard. I will also use position to my advantage. If no one raises my big blind, I will typically raise it big no matter what I am holding, since I know my opponents are weak. By doing this, I cause my opponents to become extremely cynical, and they realize that they have to take a stand. When they do, they will usually do so from a defensive posture, that is, instead of raising themselves, they will call. They think I have nothing (rather than the slight edge I believe I have), and they will call with very marginal hands. For example, in the last ten sit and go tournaments I have played, I have won the following times with these hands: went all-in with K-J and was called by K-9, went all-in with a straight on the flop and was called by two *overcards*, and went all-in with Q-10 and was called by 7-8. Sure, occasionally, you will run into a superior hand, but I find the risk/reward is well worth it. The times I win by being aggressive completely outweighs the few times that I get in trouble.

The last sit and go I played went like this: I was playing conservatively at the beginning and was just picking up enough chips to stay afloat. By the time we got down to four players, I was last in chips. The chip leader had been playing fairly well. He was also playing fairly tight but was still paid off when he made some monster hands. He was not using his stack, though, to bully his opponents. At that point, I started making my move and became extremely aggressive. By the time we were down to three players, I had almost as many chips as the chip leader. The third player was extremely short stacked when the following sequence happened: Our short stack had about $400 in chips. The chip leader had about $5,500, and I had about $4,000. The blinds were $100–$200. The chip leader was on the button and folded. I was in the small blind and found Q-4 off-suit. Now the small stack had just posted his $200 in the big blind leaving him with only $200. I thought he would call no matter what at this point. Yet, he had been playing extremely tight as his stack dwindled. He seemed oblivious to the fact that he was being blinded out. Rather than raise to $400 to put him all-in, I just said, "I'm all-in."

Now the net effect is the same. Either way, our short stack only has to call his last $200. But the psychological effect of saying all-in as opposed to just raising $200 can be devastating. On a subconscious, or even conscious, level many players are more likely to give you credit for a hand. That's exactly what happened here. As much as our short stack recognized that he should call with any hand, he just couldn't bring himself to do it. He actually folded the hand.

The next hand, our short stack was now in for $100 in the small blind. Our chip leader was in the big blind. I am on the button and find pocket Queens. Again, I say all-in. This time, I know the small blind absolutely had to call—which means I'd have to turn my hand over. I'm content to do this because I could eliminate the short stack and set up the chip leader. I wanted him to see my pocket Queens because I planned on being super aggressive with him when we are heads-up. As expected the small blind called. Then, to my complete surprise, the big blind called. I turn over my pocket Queens. The small blind had pocket sevens and the big blind has pocket fours. Are you kidding me? He called with pocket fours? What was he thinking? At best, he was a slight favorite and at worst, he was the big *underdog* that he was.

By being aggressive at the end, you force opponents into making mistakes. I really don't think that the big blind would have called here if I had not said all-in the hand before when I only had to raise to $400. He obviously thought I was raising with anything. My Queens held up, and all of a sudden I had a massive chip lead heads-up. The next hand, the tournament was over and I was the winner.

This tournament was totally won using psychology as so many are. By being aggressive pre-flop, I not only won a lot of blinds but I wore down my opponents, who were frustrated by their lack of playing ability. As soon as the chip leader had a made hand, he threw his chips in with no thought.

Position Is Critical

Back in the 1980s when I was working on Wall Street, a bunch of us used to play a weekly poker game. The game was dealer's choice, meaning that we each took turns dealing and when it was your turn to deal, you got to pick the game. Most of the games were wild, such as seven-card stud hi/lo split, follow the Queen, low card in the hole is wild, roll your own, and declare at the end. These games created a lot of action but luck was prevalent. The wilder the game, the more that luck is involved.

Whenever it was my turn to play, I chose a game called 5½ and 21½. The way this game was played was that every player was dealt one down card and then one up card. Each card had a point value with face cards counting as ½ a point and every other card counting as its face value. Aces could be worth 1 or 11. The players closest to 5½ and 21½ points would split the pot. There was an initial betting round after the first two cards, and then each player would be asked if he wanted another card. Another betting round would follow. This would continue until you went around the table and no one wanted another card. You could decline a card on one round and take one in a later round. As you can imagine, you could end up with a lot of rounds of betting. Couple that with the fact that if somebody made an exact low or high, they would be betting and raising every round. Thus, the game could be very expensive.

For instance, if you were dealt a 5 and a King, you would have 5½ points, and all you had to do was sit back and bet and raise and hope that the game went on for quite some time. If you were dealt a 5 face up, you had an excellent bluffing possibility since there were twelve face cards that could complete your low hand. Of course, it was extremely risky to bluff from early position because if you declined a card and everyone behind you did as well, you would not have a chance for another card. Being in late position was a tremendous advantage. You were able to see how everyone acted before you. If everyone took a card before the action got to you and they were obviously going high, you could lock in the low with a mediocre hand.

The way the game worked is that the dealer always had position. He would act last in every single round. I used to clean up in this game. I cleaned up so much that no one else ever wanted to call the game. What the other players failed to realize was that I cleaned up because I had position. What they should have been doing was calling the same game when it was their turn to deal. Then they would have had the big advantage. They thought that my advantage was in the game itself, and they failed to realize that my real advantage was position.

Hold'em is a positional game. Playing from late position is a huge advantage. The failure to take full advantage of position is critical to success. In the home game I play, most of the other players fail to grasp the significance of position.

In a recent game, I was on the button when three players before me limped in. I gladly called with 2-4 suited since the price was right and I could win a big hand if I hit something. When the flop came A-3-5 rainbow, I hit the jackpot. Not only did I have the nuts, but a couple of players with aces were more than happy to do my betting for me. Needless to say, I won a big pot. When I turned over the winning hand, one of the losing players made a snide comment about how lucky I was and questioned how I could possibly play such a hand. Of course, I received a lucky flop. Hold'em is about using position to put you in a position to win. You only get the button once a round, so why would I have given it up when I could see the flop cheaply.

Even if I had missed the flop there, I might have been able to steal the pot if no one else made a hand. By the way, a few hands later, the same player who made the snide comment faced a decision when everyone folded to him on the button. He seemed genuinely conflicted about what to do before folding J-10 suited face up saying he could not play that hand. He clearly did not have any understanding of the importance of position.

One of the biggest mistakes inexperienced players make is failing to adjust their starting hand requirements when they are in late position.

We know that position is important in Texas Hold'em. It is even more important in no-limit Hold'em, and it becomes extremely important in no-limit Hold'em tournaments. Why is that? No limit is much more of an art form than limit. In limit Hold'em, premium hands have more value because you can pound away at them without fear of being trapped. For instance, if you have top pair, you can safely play if there are no flush or straight draws out there. If you are raised, you can always call down without risking too much. In no limit, a big bet would put you to the test, and you would have to worry about such hands as an overpair or two pair.

Limit Hold'em is more of a math game and value betting when you have strong hands. Drawing hands like suited connectors are not as valuable since you are limited to how much you can win if you hit a monster. Now in no-limit Hold'em, drawing hands are great to play if you can get in cheap. That can be tough from early position. In late position, if the price is right, you can play more hands since there are fewer players to act behind you. If you can hit a drawing hand, the payout can be huge. You also have the ability to muscle people out from late position. If you suspect your opponent is weak, you can bet enough to force him out. In limit, it is harder to do so.

Now in tournaments with increasing blinds and antes, position takes even more importance because at some point you will have to be stealing your share of pots pre-flop if you are going to advance. You do not have the luxury of waiting for cards. As anyone who has played the game can attest, you can hit some long dry spells. You can be card dead for a few levels. The good news is that you will always get your fair share of hands when you have favorable position. If you are getting short stacked, you have to make a move while your chips still have value. When you are looking for opportune spots, you can always use position even if you do not have cards.

Remember, just like 5½ and 21½, when you have position in Hold'em, you will have it for every round of the hand. This gives you a great chance to win some hands regardless of what you have. You get to see how your opponent acts before you act every step of the way. Jockeying for position then becomes very important. If you raise every time from the button, your opponents are sure to catch on to you. So mix it up a little. Fold a few times from the button so that your opponents think you are honest. Raise from some other late positions in order to steal position. The player to the immediate right of the button is called the *cutoff*. This position is so named because this player has the opportunity to raise and force the button out and thus cut him off from favorable position.

Use the cutoff and even some *middle positions* to your advantage. For example, if a couple of players limp in before you (or even if there is a small raise) and you find yourself with J-J in middle position, raise enough to force the players behind you out. You will now have position against the early position players.

When you're in early position, you have to be aware of your opponents. How many of them understand the value of position? Who'll make positional raises, and who will be oblivious to the advantages of position? While you generally don't want to take chances from early position, you can't get run over either. If the same player is consistently stealing your big blind, you have to fight back. Raise him every so often to keep him honest. If the cutoff is constantly raising your button, fight back. Don't let him continue to take your favorable position. Let's look at some specific examples of how position can make a difference.

This first example comes from a single-table satellite tournament: This was a ten-handed table at a winner-take-all event. We were down to five players, and I was on the button with 4♠-5♠. The player *under the gun* raised three times the amount of the big blind. He'd been playing aggressively and with only five players; he'd make this move with any two high cards. I called since I had position. Everyone else folded and we saw a flop heads-up. The flop came 10-7-2 rainbow. Obviously, this flop didn't help me. However, I thought that this was a good flop for me in that it presented an opportunity. I didn't think it helped my opponent either. Sure enough, my opponent made a decent-sized bet—as he would consistently do post-flop if he had led the betting pre-flop. When he did so, I called. Why would I have called here with absolutely nothing and no draws? Because at that point, I was not playing my hand. I was playing my position. If I raised here, I might win the pot. There was also a decent chance that my fairly astute opponent would have known that I was trying to steal the pot.

By just calling, alarm signals have to go off in his head. He has to give me credit for a decent hand, since I am not trying to chase him out. Now when the turn comes I am in great position. This is where I will make my move since that is when he would expect me to if I had a decent hand. The turn brings a 9. He checks, I bet, and he folds. Even if he had bet here, I would have raised. This is purely a positional play.

The next example is a little different: It is from a World Series of Poker Circuit event. What is different about this hand is that I am actually in the big blind. Now how can the big blind be favorable position? Let me explain the situation.

We had started this event with over 600 people and we were down to under 100. The top 56 players would be paid, so it wasn't quite bubble time yet. I was playing to win and my chip stack was dwindling. The blinds were catching up to me. At this point, I had a stack of about $4,000 with blinds at $300–$600 and $75 antes. Playing ten handed, each hand would start with $1,650 in the pot. In this particular hand, two players in late position limped in for $600. The small blind called as well making the pot now over $3,000. I looked at my hand and saw Ks-9s. Not a great hand to play especially out of position. However, while each of my opponents had me covered, none of them had a huge stack. If I moved all-in for my remaining $3,400, they would have a hard time calling. Even if one did call, I was probably not a big underdog. Anyone holding A-K would have raised and I would think someone holding a hand like K-Q would face a tough decision. I pushed all-in, and as I hoped, everyone folded.

When you are in the blinds, you have the advantage of being last to act pre-flop. That advantage is short-lived, however, since you will be first to act in each betting round thereafter. However, when I am getting short stacked in a tournament, my attention turns to a pre-flop strategy, that is, I want to look for opportunities to accumulate chips pre-flop without a battle. If that is the case, then the blinds now become favorable position to me. If I am going to push all-in, position after the flop becomes irrelevant. Now I caution that this strategy is only effective when you are getting short stacked and you are willing to risk all your chips to win a decent-sized stack.

Rebuy Tournaments

When I was first starting out, I hated rebuy tournaments. I truly thought that they were fundamentally unfair. The reason I loved tournament poker is that everyone started with the same amount of chips. No one has deep pockets, and everyone is created equal at the beginning. With rebuys, that all changes. Players can buy big stacks right from the get-go. And the worst part about rebuy tournaments is that they reward losing. The way rebuy tournaments typically work is that for the first few levels of play, you can buy more chips so long as you are even or down.

So, for example, say you enter a $100 entry fee tournament with un-limited rebuys. You start with $2,000 in chips, and so long as your stack does not exceed $2,000, you can buy another $2,000 in chips for another $100. So if your stack is $2,025, you cannot buy any more. But if your stack is $2,000, you can buy and increase your stack to $4,000. If you bust out, you can actually rebuy twice. Since your first rebuy "only" gets you to $2,000, you can still make another rebuy.

Back in the old days, rebuys were done right off the bat or as a last re-sort, that is, some players would rebuy immediately before the first hand was dealt so that they would not have to worry about being over $2,000. Other players would not plan on rebuying unless they went bust. The rebuy offered these players a second chance.

Now rebuys just seem to be an excuse to go wild for many players. I see players sit down to the table with a stack of bills with every intention of re-buying numerous times. Their strategy is to try to build their stack expo-nentially at any cost during the first few levels. The last rebuy tournament

I played was an online $200 entry fee tournament. One player at the table must have made close to twenty rebuys. He would go all-in just about every hand. Opponents would only call with decent hands, so he was either winning tiny pots or losing huge ones. Every time he went bust, he would make two rebuys and then repeat the cycle. The logic behind this strategy is that eventually you are going to win a hand and double up. Even if you are a 4–1 underdog pre-flop, you will win that race 20 percent of the time. So it may cost you some money, but at some point you should end up with a decent stack.

My attitude toward rebuy tournaments has now changed dramatically. I no longer steer away from them and actually enjoy them. I do not employ the same strategy as the new breed of wild players. However, if you get one of them at your table, they really add to your expected value of the tournament. If they are willing to go all-in repeatedly at any cost to double up, look what it offers you. Wait to call them when you are most likely a heavy favorite and you can double up at minimal risk. A number of players at our table during that last tournament ended up with enormous stacks thanks to our wild player, although I noted that players only called when they had very strong hands. A couple of times I was faced with a decision to call an all-in bet pre-flop. The first time I had a small pair and folded, since I knew at best I would be a slight favorite and at worst I would be dominated. Our wild player turned over his A-10 off-suit. The next time I was more tempted to call with K-J off-suit. Again, I folded and our wild guy turned over 6-7 suited. In both instances, I would have been heads-up against this player.

I don't regret either decision, even though I would have been a favorite both times. I am just not a big proponent of gambling that early in a tournament. I do, however, think that there are two important lessons to learn here: The first is that it is extremely difficult to call an all-in bet. Even when you know your opponent is fast and loose and playing trash hands, even though you are most likely a favorite, and even if you lose and you can rebuy, it is still hard to call. Now imagine how hard it is to call an all-in bet from a player with a conservative image when you are approaching the money and there are no second chances via a rebuy. It is extremely tough to do. It is so much harder to call an all-in bet than to make one. When you are the aggressor, you are giving yourself two chances to win.

First, your opponent can fold. If he does not, you can still make the best hand. When you call an all-in bet, you have to make the best hand or you lose.

The next lesson is that at some point in a tournament, you are most likely going to have to gamble. If you are getting short stacked, you may have to call an all-in bet when you know you are most likely in a toss-up situation. Even if you last deep into the tournament, you will most likely face such a decision at some point. There is no reason to do so in the early stages, though, unless you are in a rebuy. In a fast-paced rebuy tournament, the average stack is going to be quite large by the end of the rebuy tournament. So if you are going to play, you might try to take advantage of some of these wild players—even if it means getting into a race. The opportunity will not exist after the rebuy period, and if you do not make a move, you will be at a distinct disadvantage.

Satellites

Satellite tournaments are tournaments that offer the winner(s) a seat into a larger tournament. For example, say that you want to play in the main event of the World Series of Poker, but you have no desire to pay the $10,000 entry fee. Well, not to worry, you can enter a satellite tournament. Satellites can range from single-table events to big multitable events, which are called super satellites. You could enter a $1,000 single-table satellite in which the winner will win his $10,000 seat, or if that is too rich for you, you could enter a super satellite for let's say $400. Now suppose we get 106 registrants for the $400 tournament. That is a total of $42,400. So, the top four finishers will receive $10,000 entries into the main event and the fifth place finisher would receive the remaining $2,400. In this scenario, which is fairly typical of a super satellite, only the top 4–5 percent finishers will receive anything for their efforts. However, the top four players will each receive the same thing.

So how does strategy differ in a satellite tournament? Not as much as you think. Yes, not many players will finish in the money. However, if you're playing a "regular" tournament in which the top 10 percent are in the money, the real money is still extremely top-heavy. In fact, the top 1–2 percent finishers will be winning most of the money. I find that many players mistakenly believe that they have to play aggressively from the first hand in satellites. In our previous example, they see that only the top five players will receive anything for their troubles and that drives them. Well, let's say this same $400 tournament wasn't a satellite but a regular freeze out. The top ten finishers would win money. Yet, tenth place may only receive something like $500. And the first place finisher would probably win close to $20,000, with second place taking around $10,000. Third place then may be somewhere closer to $5,000. The point is that the top few finishers in both events will be the ones making the lion's share of the money. Therefore, the beginning stages of the satellite tournament should be approached no differently than the early stages of a regular tournament.

The big difference in a satellite comes at bubble time. While there is always a bubble effect in tournaments, it is much more pronounced in a satellite. Say in the preceding example, we had exactly 100 entries instead of 106. Thus, there would be no fifth place prize. The top four players would receive $10,000 entries and fifth place would get nothing. That's a major difference. In addition, no incentive exists for anyone to try to pick up extra chips at bubble time and no extra prize is given for finishing first. In fact, the tournament ends as soon as four players are left. Everyone's goal is identical—to survive the bubble. This makes short stacks especially vulnerable. If you have the smallest stack, everyone is hoping for your elimination.

You have to be smart as a short stack. You can't allow yourself to be blinded out, but you can't be aggressive, and you never play from early position if you are extremely short stacked. Why is that? Well, say that everyone else at the table has more than twice the amount of chips than you do. You go all-in under the gun with a hand like pocket Queens. If the other players are smart, they would each call your bet and then check the hand down all the way to the river. This would maximize the chances of eliminating you. Pocket Queens are not nearly so great when you have to beat four other hands.

Let's turn our attention now to single-table satellite strategy. In a single-table sit and go tournament, the top three players typically finish in the money, which represents a ridiculously high 30 percent of the players. In no other tournament will you find this high a percentage. So when you switch to a single-table satellite, that is a significant difference. You have to be playing to win the entire thing. Keep in mind, however, that the first-place finisher is still in the top 10 percent, which is fairly typical of any tournament. And now that top 10 percent finisher will win everything. The point I am trying to make is that you have to be more aggressive in these satellites but not as much as many players think. I can illustrate this from two single-table satellites I played recently at the U.S. Poker Championships.

In the first one, one player got off to a torrid start. He eliminated five other players in the first few hands. The deck just ran over him. In one hand alone, he eliminated three opponents. This guy got off to an enormous chip lead. He had six times my stack before I even played a hand. Yet, I was not at all worried. In fact, I liked the development. From what I could tell, our chip leader was more lucky than good. He was playing extremely loose and had the good fortune of running into some other players who felt they had to be extremely aggressive from the first hand.

The way I looked at it, I was now five steps closer to winning this event without doing a thing. Now even though I did not think our chip leader was all that good, he still had a decent understanding of the game, and you don't want to give anyone that much of a chip lead. I felt confident, though, that if I could last long enough to play heads-up with him, I would have a decent chance of winning. I also knew that I would have to pick up some chips by the time we were heads-up if I were to have any chance.

So I stayed patient, and I could sense that the other remaining players (besides our chip leader) had a sense of helplessness. I waited for a couple of them to make mistakes and took their chips. Sure enough, the tournament came down to a contest between our early chip leader and me. By the time we were heads-up, he still had me out chipped by over 4–1. Yet, I remained confident. He was playing extremely loose, and all I had to do was double up once and we would be close to even.

My opponent was playing fairly predictably at this point. He would limp in with anything, and he would raise with any above-average hand. It did not take me long to pick a spot. I limped in with A-10. The flop came 3-7-10. He caught a piece of the flop with his 5-7, and he put me all-in. A short time later, I had him covered when the following hand came up. I limped in with J-6 from the button. He checked his option and we took a flop. The flop came K-6-2. He immediately went all-in. Now if I called and lost, I would be out chipped by over 5–1. However, I was fairly certain I had the best hand. He had been raising pre-flop with any King or ace. Also, he would bet aggressively post-flop with any piece of the flop. I put him on a pair of sixes or a pair of twos. If he had a six, I was also fairly certain I had him outkicked. Since he would have raised with a King or ace, the Queen was the only card he could have had that would have beaten me. The only hands he could have that would have me beaten were Q-6, 2-6 or possibly 7-7, although I think he would have raised pre-flop with pocket sevens. I called and he turned over J-2. I had him dominated and won the tournament.

The next tournament was also a single-table satellite held at the U.S. Poker Championships. This was a $50 buy-in in which the winner would win a $500 voucher (called a lammer) good toward the entry fee at any U.S. Poker Championships event. When I was signing up for the tournament, two others, players Maureen and Mark, were signing up at the same time. We struck up a conversation, and I learned that both of these players were playing a tournament for the very first time. Maureen loved to watch poker on television and really wanted to play in a tournament. Mark just seemed to be along for the ride and admitted that he did not know much about poker. In fact, before the tournament started he was still asking basic questions about the ranks of hands. For instance, he wanted to know what beat a flush.

Once the tournament started, I didn't think Mark would last long. He laid down the first couple of hands. Maureen, on the other hand, was playing and fighting. She was staring people down and asking questions of her opponents as if she were at the final table of the World Series. I'm not sure she could pick up any tells with her tactics, but she was obviously enjoying herself. After all, poker should be fun. It's a lot more fun when you win, but you're not going to win all the time.

Watching Maureen play was refreshing. Here was someone who was going to have a fun time no matter what. She was playing to win, but the experience was just as important to her. That's the beauty of tournament poker. Anyone can play, and you know ahead of time exactly how much it's going to cost you. For the recreational player, you can use your discretionary income to play, but it's an inexpensive hobby. You also have the chance to win some money. Let's look at the financial differences between playing a tournament and a cash game. Say you have $100 to spend. Your choices are to sit down to a $2–$4 limit Hold'em game or enter a $100 tournament. The $100 tournament will have approximately one hundred players and will take about five hours to complete. The top ten places will finish in the money ranging from a first-place prize of $3,600 to a tenth-place prize of $180. So for five hours of work, you have the chance to win up to $3,600.

In a cash game, you are doing well if you average one big bet per hour. So if you played for five hours at the $2–$4 game, you would be doing well if you ended up winning $20 (five hours of play at a four dollar per hour win rate). The upside is not nearly the same. That is why new players, such as Maureen and Mark, are drawn to tournament poker.

Unfortunately, Maureen didn't last long at our satellite. Mark, on the other hand, was doing extremely well. The rest of the table knew he was a complete novice. However, rather than outplay him, they were giving him their chips. He knocked three people out early on. In the first hand, the flop came J-J-3, and Mark had pocket threes giving him a full house. His opponent had K-J (for trip Jacks), and put all the money in the middle. I don't really blame Mark's opponent here.

On the next hand, the flop came K-K-5. There was a lot of betting and raising back and forth between Mark and one opponent. It was obvious to me that they both had a King. The turn came a 2. Mark made a small bet, and he was called. The river brought a 10, and Mark made another small bet. At this point, his opponent pushed the rest of his chips in, which Mark called. Mark had K-9 and his opponent had K-3. Mark had him out-kicked and won the pot while eliminating another opponent. I have no idea what his opponent was thinking. Mark had thrown him a lifeline by not putting him all-in, and instead of taking it, he hung himself with it. He had to know he was outkicked.

Mark got lucky here, but he still played those hands well and he was avoiding mistakes. He was not getting involved in pots where he did not have anything until the following hand came up. Mark was heads-up with another opponent when the final board read A♥-9♥-7♥-5♣-2♥. Mark's opponent had led the betting each step of the way, and Mark had called. On the river, Mark's opponent pushed all-in and Mark called again. Mark's opponent had 8♠-9♠ and tried to steal the pot at the end. With four hearts on board, he knew it would be impossible for Mark to call without a heart. Well, he was wrong. Mark turned over two black Jacks and scooped the pot. Now I would like to say that Mark had a great read on his opponent here but, of course, that was not the case. At the very least, he should have given his opponent credit for having an ace. When asked about the flush possibility after the hand, Mark replied that he kept forgetting about that.

By this time, Mark had an enormous chip lead—which was fine with me. I was happy that players were being eliminated, and I knew that Mark would falter soon enough. However, I could not afford to play heads-up with Mark without winning some more chips. Soon enough, we were down to three people—Mark, a third player who I would categorize as very solid—let's call him Mr. Solid—and me. Mark still had a commanding chip lead.

The following hand then came up. I was in the small blind when Mr. Solid raised from the button. I called with K-9 suited and Mark folded. The flop came 9-J-3 rainbow. I bet out and Mr. Solid called. At this point, I thought that Mr. Solid had either a Jack, two overcards, or a straight draw. The turn card brought a King. My initial reaction was positive and I reached for my chips. Yet, before I made a bet, I thought long and hard about what to do here. If my opponent had a hand such as A-K or K-Q, I was probably going to win a lot of money here. On the other hand, if he had K-J or Q-10, I could lose a lot of money here. Now usually the best way to define an opponent's hand is by betting into him and then judging how he reacts. So that is exactly what I did. I made a pot-sized bet and he responded by moving all-in. Now what?

The problem with my strategy here is that there is a good chance Mr. Solid would make this same move with A-K, K-Q, K-J, or Q-10. I determined that there was a 50 percent chance I was beat. The pot was fairly large at this point, and we each had roughly the same amount of chips. I figured if I was going to take Mark on heads-up, I had to win this pot, so I called. Mr. Solid had Q-10 making a straight, and I was eliminated when the river brought no help.

In hindsight, I realized that the only way I could have avoided going broke here was by checking the turn. Mr. Solid had been value betting his big hands the entire game. With his straight, he would have made some smaller bets in order to keep me in, and I could have called him down. When I made a big bet, however, Mr. Solid sensed I was pot committed and pushed all-in.

When Mr. Solid and Mark played heads-up, Mark had over a 5–1 chip lead. Just as I expected, though, Mr. Solid got to work quickly and chipped away at Mark's lead. It did not take Mr. Solid long to take the lead and ultimately win.

In my book *Machiavellian Poker Strategy*, I go into great detail about how there are two ways to become the ruler of the table. I won't repeat them here but will offer a quick summary. First, a player can earn his way there by playing well and doing all the things necessary to control his opponents and the table. Or a player can get some short-term luck. As you might expect, the first type of player is a much more formidable opponent. The key is being able to recognize which type of player you are up against and making the appropriate adjustments. Mr. Solid did that in this case. Those opponents who gave their chips away to Mark did not.

Hand Analysis

Maximizing Profits

The overwhelming popularity of no-limit Hold'em poker tournaments has been a boon to poker players everyone. However, the sheer number of players registered in an event should force everyone to examine their play whenever they sit down to the felt. For an example, let's take a look at the World Series of Poker Circuit, which just finished its first year.

The World Series of Poker Circuit was a series of five poker tournaments held in different cities throughout the first half of 2005 leading up to the World Series itself. The Circuit was established to leverage the World Series of Poker brand and provide more programming to ESPN. For players, it was yet another opportunity to play in top events. Much of the attention of these tournaments is always focused on the main events that usually require a $10,000 entry fee. Where the real change is taking place, however, is at the preliminary events. The great number of players entering these events is proving to be very disruptive to these one-day tournaments. The blind structure has to be aggressive to stay on schedule and players better be ready to adjust.

I played in the very first event of the very first World Series of Poker Circuit tournament, which was held at Harrah's casino in Atlantic City, New Jersey. No one knew what to expect. The tournament was to begin at noon on a Friday. I called the night before, and they told me it would be no problem registering, because they could accommodate everyone. Just in case, I gave myself plenty of time and showed up to register by 9 A.M. By

10:00 the tournament was sold out and they were taking registrations for alternates. We would start with over five hundred initial players and then alternates would be able to sit down in any seat vacated by a player eliminated during the first two levels.

I asked for a copy of the blind structure, and then went to get something to eat while I focused on my strategy. We would start with only $1,000 in chips. The blinds would initially be $25–$25 and would go up every thirty minutes. This was going to be a very aggressive structure. There would be a premium on accumulating chips earlier. However, with this many entries, the tournament has a way of slowing down in later rounds. Since so many players will be eliminated in the first few levels and replaced by alternates, there would be a lot of chips in play for those surviving.

To be in good shape at those later levels meant I would have to take advantage of every opportunity to win chips early on. Typically, I am more concerned with not making a mistake in the early stages than I am about getting every last chip. While I did not want to be foolish, I knew the structure would require me to maximize every opportunity. If not enough opportunities presented themselves, I would have to get aggressive.

Fortunately for me, I was given a chance very early to win some chips. I won a small pot the very first hand. I folded the second hand, and then on the third hand I was dealt pocket sixes in early position. I could already sense that everyone at the table was still in that early-tournament stage in which they would proceed very cautiously. So I decided just to limp in with my sixes hoping to get a few other limpers and then flop a six. Everyone folded to the player on the button who limped in for the $25. Both blinds checked (the blinds were $25–$25), and we saw the flop 4 handed.

The flop came 10-6-3 rainbow, which was almost a perfect flop for me. With middle set and no flush draws, my focus now turned to how I can maximize my profit here. The blinds checked and I checked as well. The player on the button bet $50. The small blind folded, and then, to my surprise, the big blind raised to make it $200 to go. *Well this hand just keeps getting better, I thought*. Now the action was on me, and I took a few minutes debating what to do. I was not at all worried about taking the time to contemplate because I thought it could only help in this particular hand, since my opponents may think I am weaker than I am.

First, I was trying to think what the big blind had. I immediately discounted pocket tens because I would have expected him to raise pre-flop and just smooth call the bet on the flop. He could be holding 4-5 and semi-bluffing the *open-ended straight* draw. That would seem way too aggressive. I figured he was playing either top pair or, more likely, two pair. If that was the case, then what should I do? At first, I thought about just calling the $200. The button still had to act behind me, and I was still hoping to keep him in the pot. However, just calling a $200 bet here would send off warning signals to any poker player with an ounce of experience. I concluded that there was no way the button was staying in this hand after having one player *come over the top* and another player call or re-raise.

So now my focus was back to the big blind. How could I get more chips out of him? Again, I thought if I just call here, I am going to alert everyone. If I move all-in, I seriously doubt that he is going to want to call off all his chips with top pair or even two pair on the third hand of the tournament. So I decided to raise the minimum and make it $400 to go. I was hoping he had two pair, and he would think my minimum raise reeked of an inexperienced player playing A-10.

The button quickly folded and the action was back on the big blind. He studied me for about ten seconds and then moved all-in. I beat him into the pot with my chips and flipped over my sixes. His groan said it all. I knew he had two pair before he turned over his 10-3. The board brought no help and I doubled up.

From that moment forward, I was never in serious trouble until I was eliminated *on the bubble* in about sixtieth place. The top fifty-seven players would finish in the money. I could have easily tightened up and made the money, but my goal was to win, not just make the money. While the result did not work out for me, I did put myself in position to advance based on my earlier play. Yes, I was indeed the recipient of a very good set of circumstances that third hand of the tournament. Yet those circumstances would have been meaningless if I did not take full advantage and maximize my profit.

Make a Plan and Stick with It

I was playing at a wptfan.com tournament at the Trump Taj Mahal in Atlantic City. Wptfan.com is a website started by Andy Bloch that has attracted a number of die-hard poker fanatics willing to discuss just about any topic under the sun. Of course, poker dominates the forum but with some excellent threads discussing various strategies. A couple of times a year, the regulars get together for a weekend including a tournament. I looked forward to joining them in Atlantic City, which is just ninety minutes from my home.

We started with $5,000 in chips and antes at $25–$50, which seemed like a fairly decent structure. However, the blinds increased every twenty minutes, so while you could be patient, you could not be too patient. I quickly realized that the play was going to be very solid. There was no wild play. Conservative play with selective aggressiveness dominated. The first elimination did not take place until the fourth level, which is unheard of for a daily tournament of close to seventy players. I managed to avoid mistakes and stay at a slightly higher-than-average stack throughout the first few levels. After a few hours of play, though, I was becoming short stacked. I became more aggressive and managed to build up my stack again.

I faced a critical juncture with the blinds at $300–$600 and $100 antes. Each pot began with $1,900, which was well worth stealing. I was in middle position sitting on a stack of $6,000 when the following hand occurred. Everyone folded to me and I looked down to find pocket tens. I knew I was going to raise, but the question became, how much? There were a couple of fairly large stacks yet to act behind me. They had been playing fairly conservatively, though, so I wanted to bet enough to test them. I did not want to give them a chance to play a hand like A-J or K-Q. I wanted to bet enough so that if they called or raised, I knew I was in trouble and I could re-evaluate, that is, I wanted to leave myself enough to play with in case I had to throw away the hand. Finally, the big blind was down to about $1,800 in chips. I knew he would be willing to play just about any hand, so I wanted to isolate him.

I finally decided to throw out $3,000, which was 1.5 times the amount of the pot. If I did get raised, I could still throw my hand away and have $3,000 to play with. Now $3,000 is not a lot, but this was a very tight group, so I liked my chances playing with such a short stack. Everyone folded to the button who looked at his cards, set them down, and then contemplated what to do. I knew he was going to play the hand; it was just a matter of how he was going to play. He finally re-raised enough to put me all-in. I was 99 percent convinced that he had a pair of Jacks or Queens, with a slight chance that he had A-K. Just as expected, the big blind called without much hesitation.

The action was back on me, and the smartest thing to have done would've been to fold my hand. I knew I was beat, and my original play all along had been to get rid of this hand if I was re-raised. Instead, I called my last $3,000 in chips. Sure enough, the button turned over pocket Queens. To make matters worse, the big blind turned over 7-10 off-suit taking one of my *outs*. My plan to isolate the big blind would've worked perfectly—I had him dominated—if not for the button finding Queens. Of course, that's poker.

The board brought no help to anyone, and just like that, I was eliminated. Now, in hindsight, I suppose I could have open raised for something less than $3,000, which would have made it easier for me to get away from the hand. The problem with that strategy is that when the button re-raised, I may have put him on a hand like A-Q and called anyway.

The real mistake I made was not getting rid of the hand when re-raised all-in. I knew I was dominated. More important, I had left myself with an exit strategy in just such an event and I failed to follow through.

Every Chip Counts

I was playing online in a super satellite tournament on Full Tilt Poker (www.fulltiltpoker.com). The top seven places paid with first place being a seat in the winner's choice of a World Poker Tour or World Series of Poker Circuit event. The blinds were $120–$240 with $25 antes. I had around $3,000 in chips, which was below average. There were about 40 players left out of the 120 who started. I was in middle position with Q-Q and everyone folded to me. I raised to $650. A player in late position re-raised to $1,060. This late position player had $950 in chips left. Everyone folded to me. It would cost me $410 to call. Now I was certainly not going to fold here. My opponent was short stacked and needed to make a move. He could be playing any pair from A-A to 10-10 or a hand like A-K or A-Q suited. I figured this was my do or die hand, and I re-raised to put my opponent all-in. Of course, he called.

Before his cards were turned over, I knew I had made a mistake. I had very little to gain by re-raising. There was absolutely no chance that he was going to fold. Even if I had him beat, there was a good chance I could win the rest of his stack post-flop. On the other hand, if he had A-A or K-K, I still might be able to get away from this hand on the flop. To put this into perspective, by re-raising I was left with $1,000 in chips. If I had just called, I would have had close to $2,000, which is still a short stack but a huge difference at these levels. It is a lot easier to get back into the game from $2,000 than $1,000.

Sure enough, my opponent had K-K. To make matters worse, the flop came A-K-3. That is probably the one flop I could have gotten away from if I had just called pre-flop. I made a careless mistake that cost me an extra $1,000 in chips with little to gain. I think my mistake here is a common one. We make our mind up that we are going to take a stand on a hand and then get carried away and lose control rather than maintaining discipline. I also think my opponent made a mistake here by not re-raising all-in pre-flop. If he had, I still probably would have called and he would have won my stack. By not raising all-in, he gave me an opportunity to save some chips, which I failed to take advantage of. He also opened the door for an ace to see the flop, which could have been disastrous for him. The pot was plenty big when it was his turn to act, so there was no need to get cute. Fortunately for him, though, it worked out very well.

Playing a Large Stack

Having a big stack in a tournament provides you with a huge advantage. You can bully people out of pots. Opponents are less likely to enter pots against you. You can see a lot more flops and you can take a lot more risks. However, having a large stack is not a license to do anything. With that big advantage comes responsibility. I see many players blow their stacks taking needless chances. As the blinds and antes increase and the smaller stacks become more desperate, a large stack can become a small one in one or two hands. Unfortunately, I have experienced that too often when I could have avoided the problem.

The very first time I played a no-limit event at the U.S. Poker Championships, I was the chip leader when we got down to the final two tables. With about 16 players still left (out of over 300 who started), I was sitting in the big blind when disaster struck. Two players in middle position limped in as did the small blind. I had J-8 off-suit, so I just checked and we saw the flop four handed. The flop came J-6-2, giving me top pair. The small blind bet out. Now the small blind had been playing super aggressive, and I figured he would make that bet with any pair. I thought I had him beat, but I was still worried about the players behind me. I did not want to give them the opportunity to raise it up, so I raised hoping to force them out. And just as I had planned it, the players behind me both folded. What I had not planned on was that the player in the small blind would re-raise me and push his entire stack in. Now I easily had him covered, but if I called and lost, I would go from the chip leader to a below-average stack. This situation required some careful and deliberate contemplation. Instead, I called immediately without any hesitation or thought. My opponent turned over Q-J and I was drawing extremely thin. When a Queen came off the turn, I was *drawing dead*. Just like that, I went from chip leader to the middle of the pack. Worse, I doubled up the most aggressive player at the table. He now had the largest stack at our table and began bullying everyone around.

As for me, the heavy blinds and antes starting chipping away at my stack. I soon found myself dangerously close to becoming short stacked. Our table was down to six people when I received A♠-6♠ and pushed all-in from under the gun. The rest of the table was playing very tight save for our aggressive villain who was in the big blind. I hoped everyone would fold to him and he would call with a weaker hand. That is exactly what happened. Everyone folded to my nemesis who called. When he turned over 6-5 off-suit, I was feeling good. That feeling did not last long, though, because a 5 came on the flop. I did not improve and I hit the rail in thirteenth place.

That one really stung. I had played excellent poker for over twelve hours, and I believed I was ideally situated to make a run at first place. In fact, I had made one of the best calls of my life just a few hours before. We were on the bubble—down to 28 players when the top 27 would get paid. I was in the big blind and called a bet with K-9 suited. I saw the flop heads-up and the flop came K-J-3. I bet out, and then I was called. The turn brought a blank. I bet out again and was called. Now I was really worried about being up against a bigger King. I thought I may be up against a straight draw, and maybe I did not bet enough to chase him out. When the river brought a blank, I checked this time because my opponent had a much larger stack. After I checked, he pushed all-in. This really put me to the test. The player to my immediate left was down to his last chip and would be all-in the next hand. If I called and lost, though, I would be the bubble boy. We were playing hand for hand at this point, so the entire tournament field was watching and, of course, hoping I would call and turn over a loser. If I folded, I was in excellent shape to make the money. I was not in very good shape, though, to advance far beyond that.

I took my time here and replayed the entire hand. What hand would my opponent have raised with pre-flop and just called the flop and turn? The all-in bet on the river was almost a guarantee considering the circumstances. He knew we were on the bubble and I would have a hard time calling. He sensed weakness on my part and attacked. I finally put him on A-Q. I was playing to win here, so I called, and sure enough he had A-Q.

Now if I had only given that much thought to my J-8 hand. The risk/reward ratio for me to call with that hand just did not make sense. If I had folded that hand, I would still be one of the chip leaders. By calling, I not only put a huge dent in my stack but I doubled up a formidable opponent who was on the ropes.

Avoiding mistakes is critical to tournament success. One mistake can mean the difference between elimination and big money. During the course of a long day, you require a great deal of stamina to maintain your focus and discipline. One thing I learned is that unless I have the nuts, I'll always take the time to deliberate before calling an all-in bet. At that point, since my opponent is already all-in, I don't have to worry about giving tells. I can't find any reason not to take the time, even if I am fairly certain as to what I am going to do.

Now let's look at another late tournament situation where I had a brain cramp. In this one, though, I actually gave my bad move some thought.

Here was the situation: I was playing a weekly tournament at the Mirage in Las Vegas. We started with about 150 people and we were down to the final table. Two players had already been eliminated, so there were only seven of us left. I was the chip leader and in very good shape. I had about $70,000 in chips when the player under the gun pushed all-in. This player only had about $15,000 left. I was in middle position, and I looked down and saw pocket tens. My decision now was whether to call or raise. I thought about raising in order to isolate the early position *raiser*. I figured him for a hand such as A-K or A-Q. But on the one hand I thought if I raised, I would only get called by a better hand behind me. On the other hand, if I just called, nobody was probably going to call anyway unless he had a better hand. The $15,000 was a good part of everyone else's chip stack.

So I just called. Everyone folded in turn to the player in the small blind. He thought long and hard about what to do. He knew I had him covered. After a few minutes, he finally re-raised all-in. This player had about $45,000 in chips. So now it cost me another $30,000 to call. If I lost, I was down to $25,000 in chips. If I folded, I was still sitting on $55,000. Furthermore, I just absolutely knew the re-raiser had pocket Jacks. Even if I folded my hand, I was going to get to see his hand because he would be all-in with the original player. It should have been an easy fold. I knew this, yet I called anyway. Sure enough, he turned over Jacks and I lost the hand. I ended up finishing in fifth place.

Why did I call this hand? I wish I had a good answer. I didn't trust my instincts, for sure. More important, I didn't play smart poker. I was in fine shape with $55,000. There was no reason to risk my chip position in this spot. I played extremely well for over six hours, only to blow it with one bad call.

Finally, let's look at a hand from a weekly tournament at The Borgata in Atlantic City. We were down to the final two tables. I was the chip leader of the tournament, and I was sitting in the big blind. I had about $80,000 in chips. Average stack was about $40,000. The blinds were $300–$600 with $100 antes. I was sitting in the big blind with Q-10 when there was one limper from middle position. Everyone folded to me. I checked and the flop came Q-9-3. I bet $2,000, and my opponent moved all-in for about $19,000 total. Now if my opponent had any more chips, I would have folded here. However, I was not sure if he was making a move. Since he only limped pre-flop, I didn't put him on an overpair or even A-Q. He could have had K-Q, Q-J, or even J-10. I finally convinced myself he had J-10 and was jamming with his open-ended straight draw. So I called, and he turned over A-A.

I did not improve and my stack went from $80,000 to about $60,000. I lost an extra $17,000 that I did not need to lose. I think the mistake I made here is as common as it is apparent. When you have a big chip lead late in a tournament, there is a tendency to call bets from smaller stacks that you should not call. If my opponent had $10,000 in chips or if he were in danger of being blinded out, then it would have make sense to call. Neither was the case here. I squandered chips that I never would have if I had not been the chip leader.

Being the chip leader has special privileges, and you have to use your position to bully others. You still want to use those chips on your terms, though. If you have a tendency to play loose with chips in these situations, then take the time and ask yourself before every move if you would make this move if your stack were 25 percent smaller. This should keep you from making the kind of mistake I made in this example.

Critical Points

Unless you get off to an early lead and maintain a chip advantage through-out, you are going to face a number of critical points all through a tournament. These are hands that test your mettle and make or break you. You are not going to win them all, but if you are not facing enough critical hands, then you are probably playing too passively. Being blinded out and then being forced to go all-in is not an example of a critical hand. A critical hand is one in which you are engaged with an opponent and you need to make a decision whether to force the action or retreat. Let's look at a few examples.

Full Steam Ahead

I was playing in a Trump Classic event in Altantic City and the blinds were $100–$200. I had about $2,400 in chips and the average stack was around $4,000. I was not short stacked yet, but I was looking for an op-portunity to get aggressive and accumulate chips. I was in the big blind when five players in front of me limped in including the small blind. If I could get a decent hand, I would make a big raise because there was now over $1,000 in the pot. Instead, I found 8-6 off-suit. There were two rather large stacks that had limped in that may have been more than willing to re-raise me, so I decided to check and then make a decision on the flop. I ac-tually liked being in early position here because it would give me a decent chance to steal if the flop came the right way. The flop came 8-7-2 off-suit.

I was fairly certain that no one had an overpair so I bet out $800, which left me with about $1,400 in chips. If I was re-raised all-in, I had a tough decision to make. I tried to bet enough chips so that my opponents had to realize that I might be committed to the pot, but I was still willing to fold if I really thought I was in trouble. I got one caller who looked like he was somewhat reluctant to call. I put him on two overcards or a possible straight draw or both.

The turn brought a 5 giving me an open-ended straight draw to go with my top pair and I pushed in. Again, my opponent made what appeared to me as a reluctant call. I turned over my 8-6 and he turned over his 9-10. He had two overcards and an open-ended straight draw. His 9 was no good, though, because a 9 on the river would complete my straight. The river brought a 4, and I made my straight, which wasn't needed anyway since I was in the lead.

Now let's look at this hand from my perspective about how I played and how my opponent should have played. I liked the way I played this hand. Sure, I got a favorable slot, but I made a nice-sized feeler bet and only had one caller who was on a draw. Once I knew that, I made him pay dearly on the turn. He took the bait and it cost him.

As for my opponent, I did not like the way he played this hand. First of all, I am not a big fan of limping in with 9-10 off-suit from middle position. He had a below-average stack of $3,200 and was not in a position to be squandering chips. If he had been in late position or had a bigger stack, then I could see this move. He was fortunate that no one raised behind him. Now on the flop when I bet out, he should have considered what I could be holding. Since I checked pre-flop from the big blind, I could have had anything. When I bet out, I could have been on a bluff since this was a lousy flop. Or I could have had something. Either way, I do not think calling was the right choice here. There were still a couple of large stacks yet to act behind him. Even if they folded (which they did), he should have been thinking ahead to what my move was going to be on the turn.

He had to realize that there was an excellent chance that I would move all-in considering my stack size. And, of course, that is exactly what happened. He called another $1,400 on the turn, leaving him with only $800. After the flop he was sitting on $3,000 in chips. If I had pushed all-in on the flop for my remaining $2,200, he almost certainly would have folded.

Yet, he ended up calling that same amount incrementally because he did not think ahead and allowed himself to get too involved in a hand that clouded his judgment.

On the flop is where he made his critical mistake. I think he had to either fold or re-raised me here. If he re-raised me all-in, he really put me to the test. Instead, he let me dictate the terms of the hand. I put him to the test and he failed.

Failure to Go Full Steam Ahead

The situation is a World Series of Poker Circuit event. The blinds were $200–$400, I had about $5,600 in chips, and the average chip stack was about $800. The player under the gun limped in and everyone folded to me on the button. I looked down and found A♦-Q♦, so I raised to $1,200. Both the big blind and the original limper called me. The flop came 8♠-9♥-3♥. The big blind and the limper checked. I bet $2,000 leaving me with $2,400 in chips. To my surprise, both players called. Each of my opponents had me out chipped, but neither was a large stack. The turn brought the 8♣. Again, both players checked. This time I checked as well. The river brought a 2♦. The big blind pushed all-in and the limper folded. I am almost positive that the big blind missed his draw. However, he sensed weakness on my part when I checked the turn, and he was now trying to steal the pot. My dilemma was that I did not have anything but an ace, and if I guessed wrong, I was out of the tournament. Even though I only had $2,400 in chips left, I was confident in my ability to outplay this table. So I decided to fold. I never found out what the big blind had.

My big mistake here was in failing to follow through on the turn. If you raise pre-flop and bet the flop, you should be willing to follow through on the turn. If I only had one caller, I probably would have. Both of my opponents were somewhat passive, which made it hard for me to know if they had any kind of made hand or not. Still, this was a critical point and I failed. I think I should have either gone all-in on the flop or pushed all-in on the turn. By failing to do so, I gave up control of this hand, which was a critical point for me. At a critical point, I would rather go down fighting than give up control to an opponent. Sure, I could have pushed all-in and been called by a superior hand. However, I could live with that. What I could not tolerate, though, was to be forced out of the pot by someone with an inferior hand. While I will never know, I should have erred on the side of using force and then let the chips fall where they fall.

Full Steam Ahead Too Late

This is from another Trump Classic event. We started with 152 players and we are down to about 75. The blinds are $100–$200 with $25 antes and the average stack is about $6,000. I am short stacked with only $2,000 in chips when everyone folds to me on the button. I look down and see A♠-2♠. I raise to $600, and the big blind calls. It appears to be a reluctant call, and I believe he thinks I'm trying a position steal. The flop comes A-3-6 with one spade. The big blind checks and I push all-in. He calls and says I think you have me outkicked. He turns over A-5. Now he has me out-kicked, but we will have an excellent chance to split this pot so long as a 4 or 5 does not show up in the last two cards. The turn brings the 5♠. I can still win the pot with any spade or a 4 (which will now give me a straight), and I can still split the pot if we get a 6. Unfortunately, the river is a 10 and I head to the rail.

Actually, I do not believe I played this hand too badly. However, considering my stack size, I should have pushed all-in pre-flop. I was essentially committing myself to the hand, so why not go all-in? There was an excellent chance that my opponent would fold if I did too. For me this was a critical point. This hand was one I was going to live or die with. If I pushed all-in pre-flop, I greatly increased my chances for winning. If my opponent had re-raised me pre-flop, I was going to call anyway, so I should have put maximum pressure on him. At a critical point, it is always best to apply maximum pressure. Again, I would rather go out applying maximum pressure and be called by a better hand than to play with less than maximum strength and allow someone to beat me. No-limit Hold'em tournaments require a great deal of finesse. However, at a critical point, strength takes precedence over finesse. Critical points are not the time to get cute. Give yourself the best chance of winning by playing with strength.

It Is Never Too Early for a Critical Point

It has often been said that you can't win a tournament in the early stages but that you sure can lose one. I agree that it is more important to avoid mistakes in the beginning levels than it is to take needless chances. This theory is often put to the test, though. You only get so many opportunities to win a big pot, and you have to take advantage of them no matter when they come your way.

Let me offer an example from a World Series of Poker Circuit Event: We started with only $1,500 in chips. However, the blinds did not increase dramatically and each level lasted fifty minutes. While this was not a generous structure, there was no need to panic either. I liked my table and thought I had a decent read on everyone present. We were in the second level when the following hand came up. The blinds were $25–$50 and I had about $1,700 in chips. A solid player in early position raised to $200. Everyone folded to me in the cutoff position. I looked down at pocket Queens. I was fairly certain that my opponent had a big ace. I was also fairly certain that he would fold anything other than K-K or A-A if I made a nice raise back. I decided to re-raise for two reasons: First, I wanted to keep him from seeing a flop with an ace. Next, if he did have K-K or A-A, I wanted to find out about it now. A ragged flop like 9-6-2 could be disastrous for me if he had K-K or A-A, because I could have a hard time getting away from my pocket Queens.

So I raised to $600. The next player to act was the button. The button had been playing extremely aggressively and was the chip leader of the table with about $3,000 in chips. He was not reckless, however. The button had been very selective in being aggressive. With the action on him, I could tell that he had a hand and was contemplating what to do. I really think he was debating whether to fold, call, or raise. Thus, I put him on a decent hand but not a great hand. I thought he might have pocket tens, pocket Jacks, or A-K. He did not deliberate more than a few seconds before he went all-in. The early position player folded, meaning my original read on him was correct.

However, now I faced a much more difficult situation. If I folded, I was down to $1,100 in chips, which was still plenty to work with at these levels. I also liked my chances at this table. If I called and won, I would have over $3,500 in chips and would be the chip leader of the table. Just as important, I would seriously hurt the stack of the aggressive player who had position on me. Even though this was an early stage of the tournament, I clearly was at a critical point.

Unfortunately, I did not see the picture so clearly at the time. I was still in my "avoid any big mistakes" mode. I must have deliberated for about five minutes. I was even 100 percent sure that my opponent had pocket Jacks, yet I finally folded. I was just not ready to risk my tournament life while I still had chips to work with and a favorable table. As soon as I did so, I regretted it.

My opponent asked me if I had A-K, and I said no. I told him I had a pocket pair. He said he had pocket Jacks. Now he certainly could have been lying. However, the fact that he asked if I had A-K to me was a sure sign that he had a pair less than aces or Kings. Whether he was telling me the truth or not is irrelevant. The fact is that this was an aggressive player who I had a good read on. I was not going to get many chances at him since he was seated to my immediate left. Under the circumstances, I should have recognized that I was at a critical point and should have called.

Know Your Opponent's Critical Point

As important as it is to recognize your own critical points, it is equally important to recognize your opponents' critical points. You must be acutely aware of their chip stack size and their temperament.

Some opponents are willing to be blinded out rather than move all-in with anything less than aces. Others will strike while their chips still have force. Eliminating small stacks is a great way to pick up chips at minimal risk. I try to isolate and attack small stacks whenever I have a strong hand. Even if I just have a mediocre hand, I will isolate and attack if given the opportunity. For instance, say I have pocket fives in middle position and the action is folded to me. I will raise here if the big blind is a small stack to increase the likelihood that I am heads-up with him. Unless he has a bigger pair, I am happy to get all his money in pre-flop and I am willing to gamble that he does not have a bigger pair.

Let's look at another example: Again, the big blind is sufficiently short stacked to the point that he can't hurt me that badly if I lose to him. This time I'm in the small blind and everyone folds to me. I have 8-J off-suit. I'm going to raise enough to put my opponent all-in. You have to be very careful, however, with small stacks. I'll be extremely aggressive if his stack can't do irreparable harm to mine. On the other hand, if his stack is large enough to put a nice-sized dent in mine, I'll be careful about raising him with anything less than a strong hand because at some point he's going to take a stand and push all-in.

How I decide what to do is based on a culmination of experience and my read of the opponent. The main factors I consider are the size of my chip stack, the size of my opponent's stack, the size of the blinds, the reaction my opponent is likely to have, the other potential players who may be in the pot, and, of course, my cards.

A Lesson from Limit

At a World Series of Poker $2,000 Limit Hold'em event, I went from being one of the table chip leaders to having a short stack in a matter of two hands. Remember, limit poker is just what it says. Your bets are limited to a specific size for bets, raises, and calls. You cannot make a smaller or larger bet. That said, let me set the stage: The limits were $50–$100 (with $25–$50 blinds). I was on the button and a player in early position open raised for $100. A tight player behind him re-raised for $150, and Barry Greenstein (one of the best poker players in the world) in late position re-raised to make it $200 to go. Because there had not been too many pots with multiple raises pre-flop, I was not going to get involved in this hand unless I had a monster. I peeked at my cards and, lo and behold, I had two black aces. I was happy to cap the betting at $250. The initial raiser folded (wisely), but the other two players called, meaning we would see the flop three-handed. The flop came 9-8-3 with two hearts. The action was checked to me and I bet out $50. The tight player folded and Barry called me. At this point, I put Barry on another high pair such as Kings or Queens or possibly A♥-K♥. The turn brought the Q♥. This was not a card I wanted to see because it could have given Barry a set or a flush. Barry checked, I bet and Barry check-raised me. At this point I knew I was most likely beat, but I did think there was a chance Barry had pocket Kings with one of them the K♥. So I called. The river brought a blank. Barry bet out and I called. Barry turned over pocket eights giving him a set and I mucked my hand. That hand cost me $600 in chips.

The next hand I was dealt pocket Kings in the cutoff. The player to my immediate right who had been playing very aggressively open raised for $100. I immediately re-raised forcing out the blinds and the aggressive player called me. The flop came 10-6-3 rainbow. My opponent bet, and I raised. He called. The turn brought a 9. My opponent checked again and I bet again. My opponent check-raised me. I called. The river was a blank. My opponent bet and I called. He turned over 9-10 off-suit for two pair. This hand cost me another $450.

Now pocket aces and Kings are always tough hands to get rid of especially without a pair or overcard (in the case of the Kings) on the board. After I was knocked out of the tournament, I took more than a few minutes to analyze what I could have done differently, if anything. In the first hand with Barry, I think I should have gotten away from the hand when he check-raised me on the turn. The pot was large enough that a check-raise bluff is unlikely to work. It should have been clear to me that he was value betting. Barry had to know that I had a big pair since I had capped the betting, and thus, he knew he was ahead. I easily could have saved myself $200 in chips on that hand if I had folded to his check-raise. In a cash game, I am more likely to call here. However, in a tournament, you have to hold on to your chips when you are beat.

The second hand, however, I believe I played correctly. My opponent in this hand was very aggressive and had a mountain of chips. He had been using those chips to scare people off pots. I had seen him on more than one occasion check-raise with middle pair or less. The range of hands he could have been playing were great and I could not give up my overpair to a loose aggressive player with a nonscary board.

Now let's back up a second and look at how differently these hands would've been in no limit and how we can use the power of no limit to both protect strong hands and help define our opponents.

In that first hand, when I had aces on the button and there was a raise to me, either I was going to win that pre-flop or I was going to be up against one other opponent who I had dominated. What's interesting about that hand is that I probably would've ended up heads-up against the player who saw the flop and then folded. He was playing extremely tight and my guess was that he had A-K. In limit, it's extremely difficult to protect your hand. I could only make one more raise by the time the action was on me, and, of course, Barry was going to call me with his pocket eights.

Then when the flop came with two hearts and everyone checked to me, all I could do was bet. If an opponent had a hand like A♥-K♥, there was no way I could price him out of the hand. He would be getting great *pot odds* to call. If this was no limit, however, I could have bet enough to force flush draws to fold. Yet, I see many novice players bet the minimum all the time in no-limit play. Betting or raising the minimum is rarely a good idea in no-limit play. Every bet or raise should have a purpose. If you are ahead, you want to make it expensive for your opponents to chase you. If you are bluffing, you have to bet enough to force others out. If you are value betting, you can probably extract more from your opponents with a higher bet.

One other critical reason stands out to get away from betting or raising the minimum. When you only bet the minimum, you will have a hard time defining your opponent's hand. The range of hands he could be playing are much greater. You are not forcing your opponent to make any tough decisions. You are making it easy for him. Why would you ever want to do anything to make it easier for him? More important, by betting or raising big, you make it easier on yourself. If an opponent calls, you will know that he has a strong hand. There are a lot of benefits to playing no limit. If you do not take advantage of them, you are putting yourself at a huge disadvantage. Think about it. If you are the type to bet or raise the minimum, you are essentially playing limit against everyone else's no-limit play. That is way too big an obstacle to overcome.

Defending Your Blinds

While we are on the topic of limit poker, let's talk about defending your blinds. I raise it here because I really believe defending the blinds is a limit concept. Limit Hold'em is all about incremental gains. You take advantage of every sliver of opportunity, and you defend against opponents' looking to exploit that sliver. For one bet, it's often worth protecting your blinds. If you're used to playing limit, you have to watch out for taking this concept with you to no limit.

No-limit Hold'em is certainly about exploiting opportunities as well. However, in no limit you are looking for bigger game. You want to minimize risk while trying to make big gains. In no-limit tournaments, you want to put your chips to use at maximum leverage. The biggest fundamental difference between limit and no limit is that no limit will almost certainly cost you more to protect your blinds. A standard raise is three times the amount of the big blind. It can certainly be even higher.

In both limit and no limit, you will be out of position the rest of the way. In no limit, this disadvantage is magnified exponentially since your opponents are not limited to the amount of leverage they can use to maximize their advantage. Never forget that Texas Hold'em is a position game. In no limit, position takes on even greater importance. There is a big temptation to defend your blinds in no-limit tournaments for two reasons: First, players are used to the concept from limit. Next, the blinds act last pre-flop. This can sometimes mask the huge disadvantage that lies ahead. Every step of the way from that point forward, the blinds will be out of position—after the flop, turn, and river.

This is not to say that there is never a reason to defend your blinds. Sometimes, you will have to send a message. You cannot let your opponents think they can steal your blinds at will. By the later stages of a tournament when the blinds and antes are high, you want your opponents to know that your blinds will not be given up to any raise. You can often accomplish this, however, by playing those decent hands you do receive in the blinds with a lot of strength. If you are not getting any playable hands, pick a time when you think an opponent is on a steal to fight back. Other than that, be careful and remember that this is not limit, and you will be out of position the rest of the hand.

How to Fight Aggression

I played at an extremely interesting table at a $2,500 buy-in event at the Borgata Open in Atlantic City. Approximately 350 players entered the event with a good mixture of top professionals, experienced locals, and a few newbies who either won satellites or were willing to risk some money for the chance to play in a prestigious event.

My first table had a mixture of all of the above. I was in seat six and to my immediate left was the weakest player at the table. However, two seats to my left was a very good aggressive local that we'll call Mr. PTW (for play to win). Even more intriguing was that to Mr. PTW's immediate left were David Williams and John Phan (in that order). Phan is one of the most aggressive and successful tournament players on the circuit. He likes to play a lot of hands aggressively, which makes it extremely difficult to put him on a specific hand in any given pot.

Phan started out playing his normal aggressive game, picking up chips here and there and getting out to an early lead. Soon thereafter, the table took on an entirely new dynamic. Mr. PTW started wreaking havoc. He was entering almost every pot, and he was always leading the betting. If Phan raised back, Mr. PTW would re-raise. Even though Phan had position on Mr. PTW, Mr. PTW totally neutralized Phan. By consistently raising before Phan even had a turn to act, he took away his aggressiveness. If Phan chose to enter a pot, Mr. PTW kept the pressure on. The constant pressure really turned the tables, and Mr. PTW built up a nice chip stack. Soon he was the leader of the table.

Now Phan was not just going to *lay down* and let Mr. PTW roll over him.

In fact, Phan would limp into a lot of pots and try to take them after the flop. You could sense Phan's frustration, though, at having to deal with Mr. PTW with just about any hand he wanted to enter. We reached one point where it seemed like every other hand was heads-up between Mr. PTW and Phan. They were both willing to play just about any hand.

Around that time, the challenge match between them turned on one hand. Mr. PTW had the chip lead and raised a pot pre-flop. Phan called and they saw a flop heads-up. The flop came K♠-9♠-7♥. Mr. PTW bet, Phan raised, Mr. PTW re-raised, and Phan called. The turn brought the 2♠. Mr. PTW checked, Phan bet, and Mr. PTW re-raised all-in. Phan called with no hesitation, even though it was for all his chips, of which he still had plenty left.

Mr. PTW turned over 4♠-6♠ for a flush. Phan turned over A♠-7♣ showing one pair, but he had the nut flush draw. The river brought another spade and Phan took the pot. Just like that, Mr. PTW went from chip leader to a small stack. With fewer chips, Mr. PTW lost the weaponry needed to play his aggressive style effectively. Phan, on the other hand, now had plenty of ammunition to play his aggressive style. All of this from a hand that Mr. PTW had been a big favorite to win.

In the hands that followed, Mr. PTW continued to play aggressively but with much more discretion. He no longer could afford to splash his chips around like he had been doing, but when he did choose to enter a pot, he came out firing. He met his demise when he raised all-in pre-flop with a pair of nines from late position. Men "the Master" Nguyen, who had recently joined the table, called from the big blind with A-7 off-suit. An ace came on the flop and Mr. PTW was eliminated. While I was glad to see Mr. PTW go, I had to admire his play. As aggressive as he was, he seemed very under control. I did not see him make any big mistakes. He gave himself a chance to win but had the misfortune of losing a critical pot when he was an overwhelming favorite. He was even a decent favorite on the hand that eliminated him. This was a questionable call from Men the Master as well because Mr. PTW had enough chips to make a dent in Men the Master's stack.

The most significant aspect of Mr. PTW's play to me, though, was the way in which he had neutralized an extremely aggressive player—Phan—

who had position on him. This is an extremely tough act to pull off, and I think you have to have the right temperament to even attempt to do so.

Let's contrast Mr. PTW's play with my own. I took a completely different strategy. My plan was to be conservative and wait for an opportunity to trap one of the aggressive players or use my tight image to steal some pots at ideal times. I managed to pick and choose just enough spots to stay afloat for the first few hours. After Phan won that critical pot from Mr. PTW, it became harder and harder to steal any pots. Phan was calling everyone even though it was hurting his stack. I knew my best shot now was to wait for a chance to isolate Phan when I had the better hand. I was on the verge of being short stacked and would need to do something soon when the following hand came up.

Phan raised from under the gun and everyone folded to me on the button. I had A♣-Q♣. I figured I had the best hand here, but by no means did I have a great hand. Phan could have almost anything, so I figured overall I was probably a slight favorite. My only two choices were to call and see the flop or raise all-in. If I raised anything less than all-in, then I ran the risk of a re-raise. Even if Phan just called, he was going to act first after the flop, and it was highly likely that he would put me all-in no matter what cards came.

I figured I had reached a critical point. Normally, I would not relish being all-in with A-Q suited pre-flop, but I did not believe I had a choice here. I did not want the blinds staying in the hand, and even though I didn't think I had much *fold equity* here, there was still the slight chance Phan would fold since my stack was not insignificant compared to his. Plus, anyone else at the table would have recognized that I had been playing tight. My mind made up, I re-raised all-in. Phan called without the slightest bit of hesitation and turned over A-10 off-suit. I had him dominated.

I survived the board and doubled up at a critical time. I now had plenty of chips to work with. Even better, Phan realized he was *on tilt* and left the table for about thirty minutes. With Phan absent, a decent amount of chips in front of me, and a conservative image to exploit, I immediately became more aggressive and began picking up pots.

When Phan came back, our table split up. By the dinner break, he was gone. I was staying slightly ahead of the game until we got to about seventy-five people. I made a position raise with pocket fives, and the big blind called by me. The board brought A-K-9 and the big blind bet out. I had to fold. With my chips dwindling away, I found myself in the big blind when everyone folded to Chip Jett (champion poker player) in the small blind. He re-raised me enough to put me all-in. I had K♦-3♦. Not a great hand but with the blinds and antes eating me up, I had to do something. Since Chip could raise in this situation with just about anything, I had to call. Chip had Q-J off-suit, so I was in about as good a shape as I could have hoped for. The flop brought a Jack, though, and I was eliminated.

In hindsight, I didn't think I played that well. I never gave myself a chance to get a chip lead in this tournament. Even though I survived the early table and outlasted both Phan and Mr. PTW, I was treading water the entire tournament. I think Mr. PTW played the best of anyone I saw that day. Even though he went out early, he was playing to win. He had some of the most aggressive players on his heels. More than that, he forced them into making mistakes. Mr. PTW had some of the best players in the world calling off their chips with lesser hands. That takes some doing. Unfortunately, things did not work out that well for Mr. PTW, but it wasn't because of any mistakes that he made. If he consistently plays that well, I am sure he will do just fine in future tournaments.

Aggression—the Great Equalizer

In the previous chapter, "How to Fight Aggression," we saw how Mr. PTW used aggression to level the playing field against some of the best players in the world. That style is not for everybody. However, everybody needs to understand how to use it. No matter who you are, you are going to face critical points in a tournament. Sometimes, you will get those pocket aces when you need them the most. Other times, everyone will fold to you on the button, and you can make a position steal. And I hope there will be those times when you have a great read on a weak opponent and you can exploit him to your benefit when you need some chips.

On the flip side, you'll find plenty of times when you're facing a critical point in a tournament, and you can't perceive an advantage. You aren't getting any cards to play. Every time you're in late position someone raises in front of you. You can't seem to get a read on anyone, yet everyone seems to be attacking you. It's during those times that you have to rely on your single greatest asset at the table—the power of your chips. This isn't a cash game. You can't take those chips with you. So use them or lose them. It's better to go down fighting than to give your chips away passively.

Mr. PTW wasn't going to let Phan push him around even though Phan had position on him. You can do the same thing. By using your chips, you can neutralize both position and skill. When you make big bets or raises, you put your opponents on the defensive. They must make decisions as to how much they can afford to risk. Of course, the ultimate equalizer is to go all-in. When you do so, your opponent knows the only way he can win is to have the best hand. There are no opportunities to outplay you.

Many experienced players are willing to see a lot of flops because they have confidence in their ability to outplay their less experienced opponents after the flop. They are less concerned with making the flop than reading their opponent to see if he missed it. Their attitude is that so long as their opponent does not make a strong hand, they are going to win the pot. That is tough to overcome if you are not used to getting into a lot of post-flop battles for pots when no one has a really strong hand. Those pots can sometimes be fiercely competitive, and it is hard to commit a lot of chips when you are not relying on the strength of your hand but rather the weakness of your opponent's.

Tournament poker is a game of constant adjustment. You have to be aware of, among many other things, the changing blind structure, your opponents, the relative strength of your chip stack, and the knowledge of how far you are from the money. You always want to make some kind of move while you still have some fold equity with your chips. Be honest with yourself about your play. If you are having a tough time outplaying your opponents or if you do not have enough chips to play a lot of hands aggressively, then it is time to consider changing gears. If you are going to make a move, then consider big raises or even going all-in. If you move all-in, then you take all the pressure off yourself and shift it to your opponent.

You have no more decisions to make, and you cannot be outplayed. Position becomes irrelevant. If you get called, the cards will get turned over and you'll hope for the best. Your opponent must have the best hand. He no longer has any other advantage. That's a great equalizer. With all things in poker, this powerful weapon is most effective when used discriminately.

Do Not Let Winning Mask Your Sloppy Play

Back in the late 1990s, I, like many other investors, lost some of my discipline. As a number of my high-flying tech stocks took off, I became looser with my investment strategy. In looking at potential investments in companies, I started caring less about the fundamentals, such as price to earnings ratios and a good cash position, and became more interested in profits. I was being rewarded handsomely for following this strategy, and it only encouraged looser investing. I became cocky and more aggressive in my approach.

Of course, you can probably guess how this story ends. My profits were wiped out, and then some, when the market turned south. My short-term success was masking the poor decisions I was making. Financial gain was masking my sloppy investing strategy.

Everyone who has played a decent amount of poker has witnessed poor play rewarded. If you play a lot of hands, you will win a fair amount of them. Even if you are sure to lose money in the long run, you will enjoy some success along the way. You may even go on a run that puts you up for a while. These short-term successes are what encourage the poor player to keep playing. He can justify his strategy by pointing to the pots he wins rather than to the fact that he is losing money overall. In fact, if the poor player is playing every hand, he will most likely win more hands than anyone else at the table. The trouble is that he will lose a lot more hands—and money—than anyone else at the table does. It is human nature, however, to remember your wins and forget your losses. This poor player can easily point to the number of pots he has won and make himself feel good about his play.

In poker, the good players try hard to maintain their objectivity when evaluating their play. Furthermore, they are constantly analyzing their play. They do not allow a few wins to mask their sloppy play. They recognize when they have gotten lucky in a hand that does not fit into their overall strategy of disciplined smart play.

I like to think that I have a fairly good discipline at the poker table. Yet, there are times when I get a rush of cards and begin to feel invincible. As soon as that happens, I am sure to make a big mistake and to be sent to the rail. Poker is a game of surface-level contradictions. On the one hand, you have to possess the confidence that you are going to win and can out-play your opponents. On the other hand there is a big difference between that thought process and feeling invincible. Confidence must be coupled with discipline, patience, and awareness. Blind confidence will never end well.

Pulling the Trigger

For me, the single hardest thing to do in a no-limit Hold'em tournament is to make a big bet or raise when I have absolutely nothing but I know my opponent doesn't have anything either. As much as I understand that my cards are irrelevant to the situation, it's still a tough thing to do. My guess is that I'm not alone.

Recently, I had an experience outside of poker that will hopefully help me put this part of my game in perspective. My wife and I own a rental property at the Jersey shore. It's been a good investment for us, and we always keep our eye on the market for any new buying opporunities. A house about two blocks away from ours came on the market and seemed to be greatly undervalued. We looked into it right away and found out that there was a complicated but logical reason for the seller's low asking price that had nothing to do with the market value of the house. We also knew we would have to act extremely quickly if we wanted this house. At this price, the house would not last on the market for very long. We put our house on the market immediately, but we would not have the luxury of waiting for our house to sell before putting a bid on our target house.

I was conflicted because it was a big risk to be carrying two houses down there even for an interim period. Ultimately, with my wife's clear guidance, I realized that it was more risky not to buy the greatly undervalued target house. So we did.

I find that there is a great analogy between poker principles and many other areas of life and vice versa. Thus, I always like to reflect on major transactions and negotiations to see how they can help my poker game. In this case, I realized that there is much greater risk in not pulling the trigger when I sense my opponents are vulnerable.

In a tournament, if you only win the hands you are supposed to, you are never going to win let alone make the money. In a cash game, you can survive by maximizing profit with your good hands and avoiding losses with borderline hands. That is just not good enough in tournaments when the action is forced because of increasing blinds and antes. You cannot be too risk adverse. I know that personally I love the safety net of having outs if I am going to make a play at a pot. I like to know I can make a flush or straight if I guessed wrong about my opponent's weakness.

That's great, but it's not going to be enough. If I know my opponent is weak, I have to attack regardless of my cards. My cards are completely and totally irrelevant. I am playing my opponent and not my cards. I can't worry about having a safety net. If I do, then I'm going to miss way too many opportunities to accumulate chips, which is ultimately a lot more risky than not taking the chance.

To help put this risky situation into perspective, I think back to that rental property now. Buying that property was a much greater risk than 99 percent of the chances I may take at the poker table. So what am I worrying about? To help gain confidence, think of all the times you made a semi-bluff, that is, you had a flush draw or an open-ended straight draw on the flop and you made a big bet or raise. I would be willing to bet that most of the time, your opponent folded. So that safety net was irrelevant.

When you do pull the trigger, keep in mind two things: know your opponent and know what is material to your opponent. If your opponent calls just about anything, then you should wait for a better opportunity. If you do think you can force your opponent to fold, make sure you bet enough that'll induce him to fold. Don't be looking at your stack. Look at his in making your determination as to how much to bet or raise.

Play This Hand

In this chapter, we are going to look at real-life hands from a variety of different poker situations. Play along and try to determine how you would have played the hand. Then we will see what really happened.

Situation One

It's a brick-and-mortar single-table sit and go tournament. The buy-in is $50 with the winner taking all. With ten players, first place is worth $500. Each player starts with $1,000 in chips and the blinds are $25–$50 to start. I'm in the small blind at the outset, and I don't recognize any of my opponents. On the very first hand, the first three players to act all limp in. I am already contemplating making a big raise in order to scoop this pot. Most players are very cautious at the very beginning of a tournament, and I want to take advantage of that. The remaining players fold to the player on the button who raises and makes it $200 to go. Oh well. The wind just went out of my sails. I have a feeling that the button is just making a move, but even if he is, he's beaten me to the punch. It's now my turn to act, and I look at my cards and find A-K off-suit. What should I do?

I had every intention of folding this hand unless I had a premium hand. Now, with A-K, I have a decision to make. I am certainly going to play this hand. The only question is, Should I call or raise? There is $425 in the pot now. If I am going to raise, I am thinking I should push all-in. Anything less invites a re-raise from the button. Even if I only raise $200, the button will probably at least call. So what have I accomplished? At this point, it is likely that the button's raise will chase the other players out, so I am not worried about them. Thus, I decide to call. If I hit a flop, I can probably get the button to bet into me. If I miss the flop, I can decide whether to make a move or let the hand go.

After my call, I am surprised to see the big blind call, as well as the three original limpers. There is now $1,200 in the pot, and we see the flop six handed. And I am in the worst possible position. The flop comes Q-J-4 rainbow. I have two overcards and a straight draw. I think about pushing all-in, but I am fairly certain someone has hit this flop holding a hand like A-Q. Even if someone is holding A-J, I am not sure if he will fold since he was willing to call the pre-flop raise. So I check. To my surprise, it gets checked completely around. The turn brings a 6. Again, I check and it gets checked around again. The river is an 8. I check again and the big blind pushes all-in. Everyone folds, and he flashes his A-7 before scooping the pot. The player on the button shows his pocket deuces and says he was just trying to steal the pot pre-flop.

I am not certain that I could have done anything much differently in this hand, being out of position the way I was—at least pre-flop. I really thought that I would be heads-up with the button pre-flop, and I could then decide what to do depending on what the flop brought. Once everyone else called as well, I thought my options post-flop were severely limited. When the flop came Q-J-4 rainbow, as mentioned I thought about pushing all-in. If I did get called, at least I had a straight draw; so I had a few outs. Considering how "passive loose" the table appeared to be, I thought I would get called. I think the only street I really made a mistake on was on the turn. Here is where I should have pushed all-in. There was really no hand anyone could have that would have been worth slow playing after the flop with the pot that big. Even if someone had a set, you would have to want to make someone pay to chase the straight. Once I saw everyone check the flop and the turn brought a blank, I should have made a move.

Situation Two
(based on a hand played by Christian Galvin)

We're playing a $100 buy-in tournament on Full Tilt Poker and there are
seventy-five entries. Down to thirty players and you are in the big blind
with Q-9 off-suit. The blinds are $50–$100, and you have a stack of
$4,600, which is slightly below average. A middle position player limps in,
the small blind calls, and the big blind checks. The flop is Q-J-10 rainbow
giving you top pair and an open-ended straight draw. The small blind
checks. You decide to check with the intention of check-raising the middle position player. Sure enough, middle position makes a pot-sized bet of
$300. You raise, making it $900 to go. Middle position immediately calls
the $600 raise. The pot is now $2,100. The turn is an off-suit King. You are
first to act. What do you do?

This is an extremely tricky situation, and I don't believe that there is a
right answer here. If your opponent has an ace, you are in deep trouble.
There is a decent chance that middle position player is holding a hand
such as A-J or A-10 or A-9. I believe he would have raised pre-flop with A-
K or A-Q. He could have limped in with something like A-7 suited, but it
is unlikely he would have called the raise on the flop with such a hand. Of
course, there are many hands he could have without an ace such as K-Q,
K-J, Q-J, or J-10. If he does not have an ace, you have him beat. So this is
not a situation where you are trying to push an opponent off a marginal
hand. You either want to value bet your winning hand or avoid losing a lot
of money to the ace-high straight. Personally, I would probably bet $1,000
at the pot. If I am called, I probably check to the river. If I get re-raised, I
fold. That will still leave me with $2,600 in chips with blinds at
$50–$100. The $1,000 is enough to bet here in that it looks like a value
bet. I think our opponent would have a hard time trying to raise without
the ace here because he would have to give us credit for having one.

What actually happened is that our hero checked and the middle position player bet $500. Now what do you do? That $500 is a real under bet
that either reeks of vulnerability or hopes at least to get some action for his
ace-high straight. I think I would call here, and that's exactly what our
hero did. The river brought a blank, and our hero again checked and so

did our opponent. Our opponent had K-Q for top two pair, which of course lost to our straight.

This hand worked out very well for our hero. Not only did he scoop the pot, but he got an extra $500 out of his opponent. More important, our hero was never really put to the test. The biggest mistake that I think was made was by our opponent. He had to bet at least $1,000 on the turn. The $500 was begging to be called by a better hand. If he had bet $1,000, he probably would only get called by the ace-high straight, and at least he would know he was beat.

Situation Three
(based on a hand played by Christian Galvin)

This is another $100 Full Tilt Poker tournament. There are fifty-four players, each with $2,000 in chips. Only ten hands in and our hero moves up to $2,500 after raising or re-raising five of the first ten pots. He takes down four of them pre-flop and one post-flop on a continuation bet. He has yet to have a showdown or show his cards when the following hand occurs.

The blinds are $15–$30 and our hero is sitting on the button with K-Q off-suit. A middle position player limps in, and our hero raises to $150. Both blinds fold. Middle position calls the $120 raise. The pot is now $345. Middle position has $1,800 in chips left and our hero has $2,350. The flop comes Q-8-7 rainbow. Middle position checks and our hero bets $225. Opponent check-raises making it $500. What do you do?

I think the only choices here are to fold or push all-in. While you never want to go broke with top pair early in a tournament, there are a couple of extenuating circumstances. First, our hero has been playing very aggressively, and there's a good chance he has the best hand here. Our opponent may think he has nothing. Next, if our opponent does hold a hand like A-Q, you may get him to fold by pushing all-in. As I said, you never want to go broke with top pair. It's a lot easier to raise all-in with top pair than to call with it. Finally, our hero will still be left with $550 in chips if he loses, so he won't go broke here. Having said all of this, I still think I would fold here. If you fold, you still have over $2,100 in chips and the tournament is just getting started. It's a close call, though, and I wouldn't fault someone for making a move at this time.

What actually happened is that our hero moved all-in, and he was called by our opponent who turned over pocket sevens for a set. Our hero took a big hit, and he would be eliminated not long after. At least he took his lumps being aggressive and playing to win. That's the right attitude to have.

Situation Four
(based on a hand played by Christian Galvin)

You're playing a multitable online. There are sixty-five players left and the top forty-five received cash. You are fourth in chips with $24,000. Blinds are $400–$800 and the average stack is approximately $7,000. You have just been moved to a new table and are seated on the button. The player under the gun moves all-in for $14,000. Everyone folds to you, and you look down and see A-K. What do you do?

This is a very easy fold in my opinion. I would think you are most likely up against a mid-pair hand. It is extremely unlikely you are up against a hand like A-Q. You are in excellent shape right now, and there is no reason to be taking a stab in the dark here just to get into a race. What actually happened is that our hero did indeed fold here.

This scenario raises some interesting questions, though. When would you call in this situation? I think you call here if either you or your opponent is at a critical point. For example, assume everything is the same as the preceding except that your opponent has around $6,000 or less in chips, then I think I would call. While $6,000 would be a hit to your stack, you would still have more than double the average stack if you lost ($18,000). In addition, the hands your opponent could be playing are far better, and there is a much greater chance that you could be up against hands such as A-Q, A-J, or even K-Q.

Now let's assume that everything is the same as above except that you have $6,000 in chips. This is a closer call, but I would still probably call. After all, you are playing to win and here is a chance to get into a race and

double up. If I have more than $6,000, I may fold here and if I have any-
thing less, I definitely call. I am not a big fan of voluntarily getting into a
race for all my chips, but if I am getting short stacked that may be my best
shot at building my stack.

Situation Five
(based on a hand played by Derek Scott)

First, let's take a look at a summary of the hand. Our hero here is nick-
named slart.

```
*********** # 30 *************
    PokerStars Game #2569619432: Tournament #12524391,
Hold'em No Limit - Level II (15/30) - 2005/09/13 - 21:29:17 (ET)
    Table '12524391 1' Seat #9 is the button
    Seat 1: brian_il (1065 in chips)
    Seat 2: slart (1550 in chips)
    Seat 4: bluey1000 (3005 in chips)
    Seat 6: cotter111 (1380 in chips)
    Seat 7: hop2000 (4025 in chips)
    Seat 8: PerrySoCal (1330 in chips)
    Seat 9: jollyg420 (3155 in chips)
    brian_il: posts small blind 15
    slart: posts big blind 30
    *** HOLE CARDS ***
    Dealt to slart [Qh Ah]
    jollyg420 said, "up to 19K"
    bluey1000: folds
    cotter111: calls 30
    hop2000: raises 30 to 60
    PerrySoCal: folds
    jollyg420: raises 60 to 120
    brian_il: folds
    hop2000 said, "vn" (very nice)
    slart: calls 90
```

cotter111: folds
hop2000: calls 60
*** FLOP *** [Qc 3s 9d]
slart: bets 200
hop2000: calls 200
jollyg420: raises 400 to 600
slart: folds
hop2000: calls 400
*** TURN *** [Qc 3s 9d] [Qs]
hop2000: checks
jollyg420: bets 600
hop2000: folds
jollyg420 collected 1805 from pot
jollyg420: doesn't show hand
*** SUMMARY ***
Total pot 1805 | Rake 0
Board [Qc 3s 9d Qs]
Seat 1: brian_il (small blind) folded before Flop
Seat 2: slart (big blind) folded on the Flop
Seat 4: bluey1000 folded before Flop (didn't bet)
Seat 6: cotter111 folded before Flop
Seat 7: hop2000 folded on the Turn
Seat 8: PerrySoCal folded before Flop (didn't bet)
Seat 9: jollyg420 (button) collected (1805)

Now let's take a minute to analyze this hand from slart's perspective. First, he calls a raise and re-raise pre-flop holding A♥-Q♥ in the big blind. So far, so good. The two big stacks at the table raise and re-raise. Slart has a very playable hand, and the price is still right to see a flop. Raising here would be a mistake because he runs the risk of getting re-raised and being forced to fold. He still has the risk that cotter111 or hop2000 could still re-raise jollyg420's last raise, but it's hard to play poker with zero risk. Cotter111 ends up folding, and hop2000 calls, so slart sees a flop three handed.

The flop comes Q-9-3 rainbow, which is a very good flop for slart but certainly not one to slow play. Slart bets $200 at a $405 pot. This bet is

probably a little light. Considering the size of slart's chip stack, I can understand his reluctance to bet more from early position. I don't think he needs
to make a pot-sized bet as typically done in the early stages of a tournament; a lesser amount will accomplish the same thing. However, he is up
against the bigger stacks, so a bet of at least $300 is probably warranted
here. Now, hop2000 calls, and jollyg420 makes a substantial raise to
$600.

This move really puts pressure on slart, which of course, is exactly what
I imagine jollyg420 intended. At this point, slart has $1,330 in chips,
which is plenty to work with. If he calls, he is down to $930, which is still
enough to work with at these levels. However, slart has to be aware that
the hand is going to cost him a lot more to see it to the end. If he calls
here, he has to be prepared to commit his whole stack. And if he is going
to commit his entire stack, then his two choices here are really to push all-
in or fold. Now, if he were heads-up, I would say that he had one other
choice. He can call and then push all-in on the turn since he will be acting first. The advantage of this is that if a card like a King comes on the
turn, he can sell a straight since he could be holding a hand like J-10
suited.

Ultimately, slart decides to fold, which I think is the right decision considering the action that has taken place. There was a raise and a re-raise
pre-flop. He bets the flop, and then he gets called and re-raised. With two
opponents here, there is a good chance he is already beat by an overpair
or a set of nines.

After slart folds is the time this hand gets interesting. Hop2000 calls, so
the action continues. If I am slart here, I have to be feeling fairly good
about my fold when I see hop2000 call. Then the turn brings a Queen, and
I am sure slart is kicking himself. Hop2000 checks and jollyg420 bets
$600. Hop2000 folds and slart is left to second-guess his decision to fold.

Well, he shouldn't. Based on all the information that was available to
slart at the time he folded, I believe he made the correct decision. If slart
knew a Queen was coming on the turn, he certainly would have stayed in
the pot. However, he still could have been up against pocket nines, and he
would have lost his entire stack. Second-guessing is human nature. Say
you fold 7-5 off-suit pre-flop in the face of three raises and then the flop

comes 7-7-5. You may have a moment where you kick yourself for folding, but then you will quickly come to your senses and realize you made the right decision at the time.

When you face tough decisions like the ones slart did on the flop, that is the time you are going to agonize over a good card coming after you folded. You absolutely cannot let that get to you, though. A good decision is a good decision. The fact that it was a tough good decision makes it an even better decision. Remember that and congratulate yourself on making a tough fold rather than lamenting over what might have been. Also, remind yourself that you could have easily gone broke on this hand, you still have plenty of chips, and the tournament is still in the early stages.

Situation Six
(based on a hand played by Travis Cabe)

This is a $24 satellite in a $200 buy-in tournament and we're on the bubble. Five players left and four $200 seats will be awarded. Fifth place will only receive $60. You have $11,000 in chips and have the third most chips. The chip leader has approximately $20,500 in chips, and the second chip leader has about $18,000. The other two players have approximately $5,000 and $6,000, respectively. The blinds are $200–$400 with $50 antes. You are dealt pocket tens under the gun and call the $400 bet. The chip leader is seated to your immediate left and raises to $1,400. Everyone folds to you. What do you do?

If this were not a satellite, I would definitely call here. However, at this point in the satellite, I would probably fold because I do not think the chip leader is going to raise here unless he has a fairly strong hand. In the best-case scenario, you are up against two overcards, and in the worst case, you are dominated by a bigger pair. In the real hand, our villain called here. (Our hero in this hand is the chip leader.)

The flop comes Q♦-4♦-2♠. You check and the chip leader checks behind you. The turn is the Q♣. What do you do?

Since the chip leader checked the flop, I would put him on a hand like A-K or possibly slow playing pocket Queens. I would bet around $2,000 since the pot is $3,650. What actually happened is that our villain here bet only $400, which I think is a weak and pointless bet. The chip leader is sure to call with any of his possible holdings, and sure enough, he did. The river then brought the 5s. Now what do you do?

Well, now we're in some trouble. That weak bet on the turn didn't help us gain any information at all. If we check here, we're essentially giving up on the hand because we're inviting our chip leader to bet at it. We still may have the best hand. To find out, though, we will need to make a decent-sized bet. At this point we could still fold and have more chips than two other opponents. What actually happened here is that our villain bet $2,400 and our hero called. Our villain turned over pocket tens for two pair (Queens and tens), and our hero turned over pocket Jacks for the winning hand (Queens and Jacks).

I do not think the bet on the river by our villain is a bad one under the circumstances. The problem is that he never should have been in that situation. He should have folded pre-flop to a big raise from the chip leader. Failing that, he missed an opportunity to bet the turn with a significant bet. If he had, either he would have won the hand right there or would have known he was beat and saved himself any further damage.

I do like the way our hero plays this hand. He took charge pre-flop but does not take any unnecessary chances post-flop. With a commanding chip lead, you want to pick spots to apply pressure, but above all else, you want to avoid risk and maintain your chip advantage. It is not your job to eliminate the last opponent. I know the smaller stacks are hoping you will, but let them do their own dirty work. They are the ones who are vulnerable to being eliminated. From your perspective, you want just to maintain your chip lead. This should be easy enough to do since your opponents will be reluctant to challenge you with anything less than a very strong hand. That is why our villain's play here is so bad. If he is going to play the turn, he should play it much stronger. The chip leader should think twice about calling because he will be likely to give his opponent credit for a strong hand since the villain was willing to challenge the chip leader.

Situation Seven

You are playing a single-table satellite online. Nine players start and only one place will be paid. Starting chip stacks are $1,500 and the blinds are $10–$20. On the very first hand, you receive A♠-4♠ in early position and limp in. The player to your immediate left limps in as well as both blinds, and four of you see the flop. The flop comes 5♠-A♥-4♥. Both blinds check and the action is on you. What do you do?

There is $80 in the pot, but this is a prime opportunity to win some more chips. I would not slow play, though, as there are dangerous straight and flush possibilities on board. I would make a pot-sized pot here, which is exactly what I did. The player to my immediate left called and both blinds folded. The turn brought the 5♣. This is a bad card for us because our pair of fours is now counterfeited. If our opponent has an ace, he is likely to have a bigger kicker. We are first to act. What should we do?

Since this is the very first hand, I have no read on my opponent. I don't think he has a big ace since he didn't raise pre-flop. So we may be able to chase him off a hand like A-7 suited with a big bet. However, our opponent is unlikely to give me credit for a big ace either since I limped in pre-flop. My opponent could also have played a hand like 5-6 suited, in which case he would have just made *trips*. Or he could still be on a flush draw. I think the best thing to do here is to make another pot-sized bet. The pot is currently $240. What actually happened is that I checked, not wanting to waste chips this early in the tournament. My opponent checked as well, which surprised me. The river brought a 9♦. If my opponent was looking for a flush, he just missed it. What should we do now?

We showed weakness on the turn, yet our opponent showed weakness as well. It's possible our opponent might have checked it down if we checked. However, we certainly invited a bet by checking. I think the best thing I could have done here was to bet around half the pot or $120, which looks like a value bet. What actually happened is that I checked. My opponent then made a pot-sized bet and I folded the hand.

This hand is an example of how quickly a promising hand can go south. It is also an example of how you have to be prepared for every eventuality. I was looking at the straight and flush draws out there and was not thinking about a 5 coming on the turn. When it did, it totally took me off guard.

Even with the advantage of playing online and being able to take my time without worrying about giving any tells, I froze. Considering that this was a winner-take-all tournament, I should have made a pot-sized bet on the turn. More important, I should have been prepared for every possibility on the turn so that I would not have been caught off guard. By failing to bet the turn, I failed to find out any information about my opponent's hand. By being out of position on the river, I was in a real bind and basically invited my opponent to take the pot.

Situation Eight

In the same tournament as in Situation Seven, we are down to five players. I am third in chips with about $2,500. The chip leader has over $4,000. Again, I am dealt A♠-4♠ in middle position. The blinds are $50–$100. I raise to $300. Both the player on the button and the big blind call. The flop comes Q♣-K♠-K♦. The big blind checks and the action is on me. What should I do?

This flop does not help me at all. The bigger question is if it helped either of my opponents. If I make a decent-sized bet here, I am really going to be dipping into my stack. If I were up against one opponent, I would bet here. With two opponents, there is a greater likelihood that one of them caught this flop. So I check.

The player behind me checks as well, and the turn is an ace. Again, the big blind checks. This time I bet $600 at the $950 pot. Both players call me. I figure at least one of them has an ace, but the other may be slow playing a King. The turn brings a ten. The big blind again checks. What should I do now?

I really don't see how this card helps me. Any King still beats me, and now any Jack beats me as well. This card helps if my opponent is playing a hand such as A♦-7♦ in that we would now split the pot. I decide that I don't want to bet in the hopes of splitting the pot, and the player behind moves all-in. The big blind folds. What should I do now?

I am not willing to risk my tournament life here, so I fold as well. Again, I got myself into trouble on the river by a previous misplay. I should have bet the flop. That would have helped me define my opponents' hands. Either I would have won the pot on the flop or I would have known I was in trouble. Playing it the way I did only got me into trouble with no real indication of what my opponents had.

In both Situations Seven and Eight, I had taken the lead in betting only to relinquish it when I did not like the cards that I saw. By giving up on the betting, I sacrificed my ability to define my opponents' hands. They may not have liked those cards any more than I did, but I will never know.

Eliminating Opponents

Every time an opponent is eliminated, all the remaining players benefit. There is one less opponent to worry about, and everyone moves closer to the money. Thus, great incentive exists to eliminate a short stack when you have the opportunity. Many opponents will encourage you to do so. A prime example goes something like this: You are in the big blind and everyone folds to the cutoff who is short stacked with $3,000 in chips with the blinds at $500–$1000 with $100 antes. At this point, the short stack moves all-in. Everyone folds to you on the big blind. You are sitting on $10,000, and it will cost you $2,000 more to call. You have 8♣-3♣, which is definitely not a good hand by any stretch. Yet, you know that the short stack could have gone all-in here with just about anything. He could have pocket aces or he could have 4-5 offsuit. Should you call?

The answer is, as in most poker questions, it depends. If you're playing a single-table sit and go and you're down to three people, then it might make sense. If you're in a big multitable tournament with plenty of players left, then it probably doesn't make any sense. To call here will cost you 20 percent of your stack. It's not your job to do the table's dirty work. Many players will criticize you for not calling here because they stand to benefit from you risking your stack. Don't be pressured into doing something stupid.

So when should you be trying to eliminate opponents? You really can be doing it throughout the tournament. The question is under what circumstances. When I see short stacks come to the table, I know that they are likely to be desperate and will make moves at any opportunity even if they have something less than spectacular hands. My goal then is to look for a chance to isolate them when I have a decent but not necessarily great hand. I want to get their chips before others do. So long as they do not have enough to make any kind of real dent in my stack, I am going to go after them. If they make a small raise and I have a hand like K-J offsuit, I may re-raise to put them all-in. If they move all-in, I will call with any pair or any two face cards if I know I will be heads-up with them. I am not going to call with garbage hands just to eliminate them and risk doubling them up.

In the later stages of a tournament, I will be more likely to call with garbage hands when an elimination makes a big difference in the money. For example, if there is a 50 percent jump in prize money from fourth to third and we are down to three players, then I will consider calling. My rule of thumb in this case is, I will call a short stacked opponent when I have garbage if I would still be in the same position if my opponent doubles up, that is, if I double this opponent up, will I still be willing to call another all-in bet from him because his stack is sufficiently short. If the answer is yes, then I call.

Another move you will frequently see is players checking a hand down when one opponent is all-in. Let me offer an example: The blinds are $500–$1,000 and Mr. Short Stack is under the gun. He throws in his last $2,100. Three players call him. They know that Mr. Short Stack could be playing just about anything and that he is a big underdog up against three other opponents. With no side bet, the players all check to the river in order to increase the chances of eliminating Mr. Short Stack. Not a bad strategy, but not one you should feel compelled to follow blindly.

I was playing in a World Series of Poker Circuit event when the previous scenario actually happened. At that point, there were still plenty of players left, and we were not even approaching the money yet. I was in the small blind when I called the extra $1,600 with J-10 suited. The flop came 10-8-3 rainbow. There was no side pot but I bet out anyway. The other two players were visibly upset with me and reluctantly folded their hands. Mr. Short Stack was playing 7-8 suited. An ace came on the turn and the river was a blank. I scooped the pot. After Mr. Short Stack left, one of the opponents "talked" to me about how I should have checked the hand down in order to eliminate Mr. Short Stack. Of course, this player had folded an ace—which is exactly why I did not check the hand down. I figured one, if not both, of my opponents had to have overcards. Why let them stick around? There was a decent-sized pot to be had and I wanted to be heads-up with Mr. Short Stack. My goal here was to accumulate chips. I was not worried about Mr. Short Stack.

I am surprised, though, at how many players think that it is an automatic check down in that situation. Knowing that, I will sometimes use it to my advantage. For example, say another player and I call a third player's all-in bet. I am first to act and I am sitting on A-10. I may "check in the dark" (which is checking before the flop is turned over) in a conspicuous manner to signal that I am willing to check it down and my opponent should as well. This is a hand I probably want to check down unless I flop a monster. If the board brings an ace, I may be betting into an ace with a bigger kicker. If the board doesn't help, I want to see the hand to the end for free since I could *draw out*. And if I do flop a monster, then my check in the dark may help me win a bigger pot later. If I do not hit a monster, I will continue to check in the dark before every card in order to coerce my opponent into checking as well.

By the way, this is the one and only set of circumstances that I will ever consider to check in the dark. Poker is a game of imperfect information. Before I make any decision, I at least want as much information as is available to me. Even if there is a strategic reason for me to check, I think it is much more effective to wait and see the cards. For instance, if I know that I want to check-raise bluff an aggressive opponent, it will be much more effective if he sees me check after I look at the flop.

Hypotheticals

Since poker is a game of infinite possibilities, it remains a game of never-ending learning. Playing, reading, and discussing as much as possible are critical to one's learning curve. While every hand is unique, lessons can be learned that are applicable to a variety of situations. However, some situations provide a much deeper understanding of the nature of no-limit Texas Hold'em tournaments. I have included a few of these as hypothetical situations. Whether these situations are likely or not, a thorough analysis of the hands will provide a deep philosophical understanding of tournament strategy overall. That understanding is sure to improve your game.

Do You Risk It All?

A popular hypothetical exists that's often discussed in poker circles. In fact, you may have heard or read a discussion about it elsewhere. I didn't make this hypothetical up, and if I knew who did, I'd certainly offer him or her credit here. If you're familiar with it, my guess is that you heard a different conclusion than the one I'm going to argue. This hypothetical presents a situation that is unlikely ever to happen. Yet, I believe it's extremely important to analyze because of the underlying lesson that has widespread ramifications of how one approaches no-limit Texas Hold'em tournaments. Anyway, that's enough background. Let's get to the hypothetical.

It's the first hand of the main event of the World Series of Poker. Start-

ing stacks are $10,000 and the blinds are $25–$50. You are in the big
blind when everyone folds to the small blind. The small blind goes all-in.
Before he does, though, he inadvertently flashes his cards to you revealing
the A♠-K♠. You look down and find two red Queens in your hand. You are
a 53.8 percent favorite. However, this situation also means that there is a
46.2 percent chance that you will be eliminated. What do you do?

The math guys will tell you to call every time. You have an advantage,
so take it. Poker is a game about finding any edge you can and then exploiting it. They will tell you that whenever you have positive equity, the
decision is a no-brainer. The counterargument is, Why in the world would
you leave your entire tournament livelihood to what is essentially a coin
flip? Presumably you entered the tournament because you believed in your
skill and ability to outplay your opponents. Give yourself the chance to
outplay them and build your stack rather than risk elimination.

Here's my point of view. Poker is a combination of math and psychology. If you are playing limit Hold'em online, then the game is mostly a
math game. That is why many successful players are able to play numerous tables at a time and win a lot of money by playing by the book. No-
limit Hold'em is much more artful. The opportunity to put your entire
stack to work at any time creates a much more nuanced game. You have
to know your opponents and their tendencies. The rift between science
and art grows greater in a no-limit Hold'em tournament. With the increasing blinds, the action is forced and players must use their skill and
cunning rather than rely on just their cards. Math is still an important factor. However, it is only one factor. Just because you have pot odds does not
mean that you should call.

Now if you were playing a sit and go tournament and you could enter
into another one as soon as you were eliminated, then I would say go
ahead and call in the preceding hypothetical. If you were playing a cash
game and could easily afford the call, again I would say it is an easy call.

However, I would assume the World Series of Poker Championship is
important enough to everybody that it is not worth the call here. Sure, you
can double up. But doubling up with the blinds at $25–$50 is not that big
of an advantage. To work with $10,000 is plenty. Look at it this way:
Would you rather have $10,000 to start 100 percent of the time or would
you rather have $20,000 to start 53.8 percent of the time knowing you

will be eliminated the other 46.2 percent of the time? Remember, this is elimination from the World Series before you have had the chance to give your skill a chance. To put it in perspective, let's look at the equivalent from a cash game. Would you risk your entire bankroll by calling in this situation? Sure, you have a 53.8 percent chance of doubling your bankroll. But is that worth the 46.2 percent chance of going broke? I would like to see the math guys argue that one.

In case I have not convinced you yet, let's look at this from one other point of view. In this example, since you are a 53.8 percent favorite and you are each starting out with $10,000 in chips, you have an expected value (EV) of $10,760. Since this number is greater than your starting and current stack amount, the math guys will tell you to go ahead and call. Yet, we know that there is no way you will end up with $10,760. In actuality, you will end up with either $20,000 or zero. If you were going to play the main event of the World Series of Poker an endless amount of times, then I would agree that you should go ahead and call. That EV becomes much more relevant. However, if you take into account that this tournament only comes once a year and many players may only play once in their lifetime, then I suggest that this edge is not great enough to risk that 46.2 percent chance of losing all your chips.

Don't Accept Every Situation as Presented

This situation is a hypothetical that I first read as posted on wptfan.com, which generated a lot of discussion:

Let's say you are in a tournament with three people left. You're by far the chip leader with $170,000 and both second- and third-place have $28,000. Blinds are $3,000–$6,000 and you're on the button. Payouts are $3,500 for first, $2,100 for second, and $1,400 for third place. Let's say your decision is to either jam (move in) or fold. What is optimal play here? What range of hands do you jam with?

There were many responses, and while everyone had his own theory as to what hands one should push all-in with and what hands one should fold with, nobody disagreed with the premise that pushing all-in or folding were the only options. Personally, I am not sure that I agree with the premise that your only options are to push all-in or fold here. Put yourself in the position of one of the smaller stacks. There is a big difference between second- and third-place money. Depending on your position, you probably have some opportunities just to limp in or raise two to three times the big blind. If you see some flops, you can probably get either player to fold if he misses the flop. And if you hit the flop, you are in excellent position to eliminate an opponent. You are in an ideal situation here. By moving in with a wide range of hands here, you run the risk of doubling up an opponent. Then that opponent can be more aggressive against the remaining short stack. Each of your opponents has a strong motivation to stay alive here. I would be aggressive but selective. I would try to trap with very strong hands. My goal here would be to eliminate one of them (when I know I have the better hand) so that I maintain a strong chip lead once we reach heads-up.

When there is a substantial difference between second- and third-place prize money, there is a big incentive for either of the smaller stacks to remain alive. With a big stack here, your goal is to win the entire thing. Granted, most of the time you will push all-in when raising. There will be times when you can make a small raise. Let me offer an example: You (the big stack) are on the button with 8-9 suited. You raise to $12,000. The small stacks will still have a hard time calling here if they have garbage. (At this point, they are just trying to outlast each other, and every chip counts.) If they have a strong hand, they will push all-in on you, and you can still decide whether to call. I do not believe it is an automatic call here because you still want to keep the small stacks down. Save your extra $16,000 in chips to make a play on a later hand.

Now I am sure that plenty of people will disagree with me here, and I do not claim to have all the answers. The larger point to me is that I think many players look at situations in absolutes or believe that there is a clear-cut answer. I was surprised that in a group as smart and experienced as the posters on wptfan.com are, no one posted a response questioning the premise. I think there is a tendency to accept certain poker principles as law without critically thinking and evaluating each situation independently.

Two Questions

I have two questions for you to answer: The first is rhetorical. How many pots have you won by calling when you did not have the best hand? Of course, the answer is none. If you answered anything else, please call me as I want to join your game. While this is an obvious question, it underscores a more fundamental issue: If you are playing a tournament and you only win those pots when you have the best hand, you are not going to advance very far. Furthermore, if you find yourself frequently calling with the best hand, you are not extracting maximum value for your strong hands.

In a perfect world, you should be either folding or bluffing when you are beat but never calling. On the flip side, you should be betting or raising at some point (even if you are trapping) when you do have the best hand. Of course, poker is a game of imperfect information, and there will be times when calling is appropriate. However, if you do it frequently, you need to take a serious look at your game to find out what you are doing wrong. If you like to play a lot of pots, then I would suggest that you play far fewer, and when you do enter, play with strength. When you take the lead in the betting, you give yourself two chances to win: First, you can force your opponents to fold. Next, you could end up with the best hand. When you are passive and insist on just calling, you have no chance to win. That second chance to win by forcing your opponent to fold is commonly referred to as your fold equity.

For instance, say you are sitting on about seven times the big blind late in a tournament. Everyone folds to you in the cutoff position, and you look down and find J-10 suited. This is a great drawing hand, so you think about calling. At this stage of the tournament, though, that is the wrong move. If you are going to enter, you should raise. This way you give yourself the chance to win the blinds and antes by forcing your opponents to fold. If you just call and miss the flop completely, what are you going to do when your opponent bets out? In tournament poker where the increasing blinds force the action, you do not have the opportunity to sit back; you must be proactive. In my book *Tournament Poker and The Art of War*, I teach players to develop the proper mindset to use their chips as leverage to gain other chips.

That brings us to the second question. This is not a rhetorical question and is one that you should answer as honestly as possible. How many times after you have been eliminated from a tournament have you complained that you were card dead? Do not feel bad if you have. I know I have done it numerous times before I straightened myself out. I still hear top professionals complain about it all the time. Well, now is the time to correct this mistake. Personally, I find card dead stories more repellent than bad beat stories. At least with a bad beat story, the narrator presumably made the right move and suffered some bad luck. When I hear a card dead story, though, my immediate reaction is that the narrator does not understand the game and that he was not proactive enough to compete.

The whole point of tournament poker is to force the action by increasing the blinds and antes. You do not have the luxury of waiting for optimal cards. Neither do your opponents. In any tournament, some players will get a rush of cards at the beginning and others will be card dead. Deal with it. However, every single player will have an opportunity to make a move and accumulate chips. If you are staying focused and studying your opponents, I guarantee that you will find some spots to pick up chips even when you do not have anything. You may not be a chip leader, but you can pick up enough to survive and avoid being short stacked until bigger opportunities arrive. Of course, there will be times that you get caught stealing. That is part of poker. However, if you were card dead, would you rather get blinded out or get caught making a move? Give yourself a chance to win. Make some moves before you get so short stacked that you are guaranteed to get called down. Take advantage of your chips to give yourself some fold equity.

It's not easy trying to win chips when you don't have cards. Making such moves is a huge psychological hurdle to get over. If you have trouble getting over that hurdle, I'm going to give you a confidence builder right now. In fact, you already know how to make moves without cards. You just don't know it. Next time you play, count how many hands you win without a showdown. Count both the number of hands you win without a showdown and the percentage of your winning hands that come without a showdown. I think you will be surprised at how high the number is. If you are playing online, just click on the stats icon, and you will instantly get all this information.

What does this tell you? It tells you that your cards were irrelevant in those hands that you won without a showdown. Actually, they weren't irrelevant because they gave you the confidence to bet them. However, assuming your opponents' cards stayed the same, you could've bet any two cards the same way and won the pot. Think about that. If you're playing correctly, most of the pots that you win will come without a showdown. Sure, it's nice to have the security blanket of cards to back up your bets, but if you're not getting cards, then you're going to have to make due without them. In those situations, think of your chips as your security blanket. Bet them to protect the hand that you don't want to reveal. So long as you have chips, you have a way to win whether or not you are getting cards.

One other thing—poker is a streaky game. If you are card dead at the beginning, the cards will eventually come. Over the long run, things even out. If you can do enough to survive the dry spells, you will be in good shape when you do get some cards at the higher levels. Every tournament I see some players get off to a quick start only to flame out quickly when the cards do not go their way. Think about it. Would you rather be card dead at the beginning of the tournament or the end? Do whatever you can to survive those dry spells because they never last forever. So do not tell bad beat stories, and from now on, you keep those card dead stories to yourself as well. Instead, next time you are eliminated, think about some situations in which you could have picked up some chips, even though you did not have cards. You should be playing poker because it is a skill game. If you are blaming the cards, then you are relying on luck.

One Joke

Two couples were playing poker one evening. John accidentally dropped some cards on the floor. When he bent down under the table to pick them up, he noticed Bill's wife Sue wasn't wearing any underwear under her dress!

Shocked by this, John, while trying to sit back up again, hit his head on the table and emerged red-faced. Later, John went to the kitchen to get some refreshments. Bill's wife followed and asked, "Did you see anything that you liked under there?" Surprised by her boldness, John courageously admitted that, well, indeed he did.

She said, "Well, you can have it, but it will cost you $500."

After taking a minute or two to assess the financial and moral costs of this offer, John confirmed that he was interested. She told him that since her husband Bill worked Friday afternoons and John didn't, John should be at her house around 2 P.M. Friday afternoon.

When Friday rolled around, John showed up at Bill's house at 2 P.M. sharp, and after paying Sue the agreed sum of $500, they went to the bedroom and closed their transaction, as agreed. John quickly dressed and left.

As usual, Bill came home from work at 6 P.M. and, on entering the house, asked his wife abruptly, "Did John come by the house this afternoon?"

With a lump in her throat, Sue answered, "Why yes, he did stop by for a few minutes this afternoon."

Her heart nearly skipped a beat when her husband curtly asked, "And did he give you $500?"

In terror she assumed that somehow he had found out and after mustering her best poker face, replied, "Well, yes, in fact he did give me $500."

Bill, with a satisfied look on his face, surprised his wife by saying, "Good, I was hoping he did. John came by the office this morning and borrowed $500 from me. He promised me he'd stop by our house this afternoon on his way home and pay me back."

Now certainly John's behavior in this joke can't be thought of as anything less than morally repugnant. In fact, his behavior is so outrageous that it makes for a funny joke. I would hope none of us ever behave in any manner similar to John's in this example in any part of our life—except one. That's right. John would make a pretty good poker player.

When you sit down to the table, you have nine opponents trying to take your money. If you are going to succeed, you have to have the attitude that you will steal from your best friend. Plus, you want to do it in a way that your opponents never figure it out. This deceitful behavior is not only perfectly acceptable at the poker table, but it is expected. And that's the attitude your opponents are going to bring with them.

It doesn't make you a bad person to have this attitude at the poker table. You just need to distinguish your poker persona from the person outside of the poker room. Putting on your poker face requires a total transformation. You have to check your everyday self at the door. Just don't forget to pick him up on the way out.

Deal Making

The similarities between poker and business are enormous. In fact, many of the skills necessary for poker are essential for business and vice versa. You would think then that poker players would make good business people or at least possess some savvy negotiating skills. My experience has been that many do not. Why is this important? Because at the end of most tournaments when only a few people are left, inevitably the discussion will turn to cutting a deal. In tournament play, your ability to negotiate a good deal is just as important as your poker skills. Tournaments reward the top few finishers. The top two or three players typically win over half the total prize pool. However, the difference between first and third is significant. For example, say there are three players left with equal chip stacks and the remaining prize pool is as follows: first place is $20,000, second place is $10,000, and third place is $5,000. That is $35,000. All things being equal, a simple way to divide this would be that each player takes $10,000, with first place getting the extra $5,000. Or if there is no reason to play on, each player could just take one third of the entire prize pool. Many events will require that something be left on the table for first place and that the players play on.

Of course, things are hardly that simple. Some players may have no interest in cutting a deal. Even if everyone wants to, there could be a huge disagreement as to how to divide up the kitty. If you are playing a satellite where a seat to a large tournament is up for grabs, things get even trickier. Now factor in that you are trying to play a tournament that requires your complete and undivided attention, and you can see that it is good to have an idea of how to cut a deal before you ever get to that point.

There are five main factors to consider in cutting a deal: the relative chip stack size, the size of the blinds, your skill level compared to your opponents, your goal, and your opponent's goal. Let's look at the factors and then address specific guidelines to follow when negotiating.

The most important factor is the relative size of the chip stacks. When you look at chip stacks, you also have to consider how many players are left and what is the level of the blinds. If you are playing heads-up and one party has another party dominated in chips, there is little incentive to cut a deal. If the blinds are already at a high level, then the chip leader is an overwhelming favorite to win, so why would he give up a dime of the first-place prize money. Now if there are three players left and one player has a 2–1 chip advantage and the blinds are still small, then there may be some incentive to cut a deal. No matter what the amount of stacks, though, never assume that a deal cannot be reached. You never know unless you ask. When you get down to the end and the blinds are high, there is a lot of luck involved. Many players are willing to cut a deal in order to minimize the effect of luck even if they are ahead.

Be realistic about your chances. Carefully analyze the situation. You have to have a lot of confidence in your ability to play poker. Whenever you sit down to the table, you have to believe that you can beat the opposition no matter who it is. When it is time to think about a deal, though, be objective. Be honest with yourself. How tough are your opponent(s). How well is he or they playing? How well are you playing? Are either you or your opponent getting fatigued?

Next, consider your goals and own personal financial situation. I see many so-called experts advocating against cutting a deal whenever you have a sizable chip advantage. Nothing is that black and white. If the guaranteed money of cutting a deal is important to your financial well-being, then by all means be willing to do so. For instance, say there are three players left and the place prize money is $100,000 for first, $50,000 for second, and $25,000 for third. That's $175,000. You have about $50,000 in chips, and your two opponents have about $25,000 each. You have a good read on each of your opponents, but you and your spouse have also been house hunting recently. You are about $50,000 short of the down payment you need on the house you both love. Now if you continue to play, you have a fairly decent chance of winning at least $50,000, but there is no guarantee. After all, anything can happen in poker.

For you personally in this situation, there is a huge advantage to cutting a deal. If you could reach a deal where you got $75,000 and each of your opponents took $50,000, then I would say take it. Why gamble with that down payment on your house?

Ultimately, cutting a deal is always a personal choice. You should never feel pressured into making one. If there are five of you left and the other four all want to cut a deal and you don't, so be it. Conversely, don't waste your time and energy trying to convince someone else to cut a deal. Not only is it bad etiquette, but it can affect your game if you're too worried about convincing them rather than playing poker. However, if you do decide you want to cut a deal, let's look at some specific negotiation techniques to help you cut the best possible deal.

Don't Make the First Offer

If possible, don't make the first offer. To take it one step further, try not to make the first inquiry. Let someone else bring up the topic of making a deal first. Once you know someone wants to make a deal, it greatly increases your bargaining power. When someone does bring up the topic, act disinterested. You don't have to reject the idea, but be noncommittal to see how much your opponent will keep pushing for a deal. If he persists, then say something like, "I usually don't cut deals, but what did you have in mind?"

Don't offer anything up until he makes a first offer. No matter what the offer is, reject it and don't offer a counteroffer. Just say something like, "I'm not interested at that price." Then wait and see if he makes another offer. Now, remember just like poker, negotiating is situational. If you really want to cut a deal and no one is bringing up the subject, then you may have to initiate it. If you do, still try to get your opponent to make the first concrete offer. Also, keep in mind that things can change quickly while you're trying to negotiate. You could take a big hit to your stack and thereby weaken your position. The flip side is that if your opponent wants to cut a deal, he's not going to want to lose any more chips until the deal is cut. You can use this to your advantage to attack him just as if you would at bubble time.

Identify Your Opponent's Goal

Imagine how easy poker would be if you knew what cards your opponent had. Of course, your opponents don't want you to know that information. Yet, when it comes to negotiating a deal, it's amazing how many players will reveal their hands. I was playing a satellite for a seat in a bigger event at The Borgata Open a couple of years ago. Only one seat into a $2,500 tournament would be awarded. Second place was only $100. The tournament cost each player about $150 to enter. This is an average since there were rebuys.

When we got down to three players, one player (let's call him Player Let's Make a Deal) suggested that we make a deal. At the time, one player (let's call him Player Open Book) had about $40,000 in chips while the other guy and I had about $20,000 each. Well, making a deal in a satellite like this is extremely difficult because the player who wins the seat would have to pay cash to the others. Not many players are willing to do this. And, in fact, Player Open Book was not willing to do that here. However, Player Open Book also told me that he didn't think he would be able to make the $2,500 event for which he might win a seat. I did not volunteer anything and we played on. Soon thereafter, Player Let's Make a Deal was eliminated by Player Open Book. Now Player Open Book had me seriously out chipped. I asked him if he wanted to buy me out for $1,000. Of course, he said no. I told him I wouldn't do it if I were him either. A short while later, I battled back.

While I was still down in chips, about $50,000 to $30,000, this time I asked him if he wanted me to buy him out. This peaked his interest. He asked if I would give him $1,000. I politely declined and said it was not worth it to me. I stated that the only reason I was playing a satellite is that I wanted to try to get in the bigger tournament cheaply. The conversation continued for a few hands, and we finally settled whereby I would buy him out for $500. So even though I was out chipped, I was able to buy a $2,500 seat for $500.

I was able to accomplish this for two reasons: First, I knew my opponent. I knew he had a high incentive to settle, since he could not make the $2,500 event. Next, he had unwittingly set the market price by declining to pay $1,000, and I, of course, had agreed with him. Even though I was out chipped, I had leverage here and I exercised it. Now I am not sure that you will find many situations quite this ripe, but if you can find out where your opponent's interests lie, you will have the upper hand.

Close the Deal

Poker is a fluid game. Things change quickly. One hand can change the entire dynamic of the table—especially at the end of tournaments when the blinds are high and only a few players remain. If you are close to a deal or have a tentative agreement, stop the action. Ask the dealer to hold up and call the floor boss over. Maybe even ask for a ten-minute break if you need to iron out the details. The key is that as soon as you think you are close to a deal that you want, make sure that the action stops. You do not want another hand played that could completely change someone's mind. You also do not want to give players time to reconsider. Once you stop the action and shake hands, players will feel honor bound to complete the deal.

The Cost of Not Doing a Deal

A recent night at the Trump Taj Mahal in Atlantic City was a tough reminder for me of the cost of not doing a deal. I went down to play in the Trump Classic. I arrived there on a Thursday night around 8:00 P.M. with the idea of playing the super satellite at 9:00 (for a seat in the main event) and then playing one of the no-limit Hold'em events the next day. Since I had an hour to kill, I signed up for a single-table sit and go. It was a $50 (plus $15) entry fee. Ten people played with the winner taking $500. I had played these before and typically by the time you were down to two people, the blinds were so high, that it made sense to cut a deal unless one player had a huge chip lead; otherwise, you were leaving too much to luck. When first place is $500 and second is nothing, that is a big incentive for even the most optimistic poker player.

I was playing this sit and go, and sure enough it came down to another player and me heads-up. I had a good read on this guy and knew I could outplay him. However, he also had about a 4–1 chip lead on me. At this point I learned that the super satellite I wanted to play had already started. So I was really motivated to cut a deal and asked my opponent if he was interested. He declined, which I would have done if I had that big of a chip advantage. After that I got to work, and within about ten minutes I took a slight chip lead. Now I felt very confident that I would win this thing, but I really wanted to get to my other tournament. I offered to split the pot 50 percent each and again my opponent declined. That really surprised me. Here I was completely outplaying him, and he wanted to keep playing. Oh well. Now my focus was on beating him.

A few hands later I had built my chip lead up when I limped in with A-Q hoping to trap him. He called. The flop came Q-9-6. My opponent went all-in, and I gladly called. He had 9-7. The turn was an 8 and the river a 5 giving him a straight. Just like that, I was short stacked. The next hand I went all-in with A-7 and am called by his K-4. He flops a 4 and I don't improve.

When all the money goes to first place, it's tough not to cut a deal. Here, I liked my chances against what I perceived to be a weaker opponent. I still offered a deal. My opponent declined. I had all his chips in the middle when I was a big favorite, and I still lost.

Now I had to put it behind me and get to work on the super satellite. I only missed one round of blinds, so I was in fine shape. The tournament had nineteen players, and first place would receive a seat in the $5,000 main event. Second place would get $50.

Obviously, this is a huge difference. There is a huge incentive to cut a deal with that kind of payout structure. The problem is that it is also extremely difficult to make a deal when you have a seat as one of the prizes. That $5,000 seat is nontransferable. The winner cannot sell it.

When we got down to three people, our chip stacks were approximately as follows: Player 1 had $35,000; Player 2 had $20,000; and I had $25,000. Player 2 brought up the idea of striking a deal. He proposed that

Player 1 pay Player 2 and me $1,000 each and then Player 1 could take the seat. While this was not a deal I would have agreed to at this point, I knew Player 2 would never go for it. If this were $5,000 cash, Player 2 would have probably jumped at the chance to keep $3,000. In this case, though, Player 2 would have to take $2,000 out of his pocket. If he did not cash in the $5,000 event, he would be a $2,000 loser. The whole reason that people played these satellites was to get a seat in a main event cheaply. There was just no way a deal was going to get struck with three players.

Soon enough, Player 2 was eliminated. At that point, Player 1 had about $50,000 and I had about $30,000. I asked Player 1 if he wanted to cut a deal. He said that he really didn't have any money to buy me out. I completely understood his position, and actually I really didn't want him buying me out. I wanted to buy him out. After a while, I took a slight chip lead. Now I brought up the idea of striking a deal again. This time, I asked if he wanted me to buy him out. He seemed interested, but I let him know it wasn't going to be for $1,000. He had already set the bar low (and I had agreed) that no one wants to pay $1,000 for a seat that you are trying to win cheaply. I then asked the floor manager if he could stop the clock on the game. He said to play the hand we had just been dealt.

I looked down and saw A-9 suited and made a nice raise of about five times the big blind. Player 1 called. The flop came 9-4-2. Player 1 checked. I was eager to get back to the negotiations and pushed all-in with top pair and top kicker. To my surprise, my opponent called. For a moment, I thought that I was going to win without having to give up anything. Then Player 2 turned over pocket deuces for his set of twos. I was in serious trouble. My hand did not improve, and now I was not only extremely short stacked but completely devoid of negotiating power. I did manage to negotiate a $100 save for whoever came out of second that my opponent was gracious enough to agree to. A few hands later, I was eliminated.

I have no regrets about how I played in this tournament. Heads-up, I am going to lose my chips just about every time with top pair and top kicker. I do regret not striking a deal when I had the chance. I should have just stopped the play and worked out a deal. There was too much at stake between first and second place.

The Business of Poker

This section isn't about the business side of poker but rather about how business strategies can be incorporated into, and help, your poker game. We'll take a look at some time-honored and fundamentally sound business strategies to improve your game.

A Look at Beta

Beta is a Greek letter. In business terms, it means variability. Something with a high beta has a high variance rate. How is this relevant? Let's say you're looking at two alternative investment opportunities. Both have the same expected rate of return. However, one has a much higher beta than the other does. If that's the case, you'll choose the investment with the smaller beta every single time. Now if the investment opportunity with the higher beta offered a potentially higher rate of return, then you may choose that one depending on your risk tolerance.

How is this relevant to poker? When you are sizing up your opponents, you should understand their beta. Some of your opponents will be fairly predictable and thus have a low beta. Other opponents will vary their play greatly and have a high beta. If that is the case, then you should concentrate on playing against those opponents with a lower beta. They are more predictable, and you are less likely to get in trouble. The only time you would vary from this is if you believe your rate of return will be greater going up against those opponents with a high beta and you are willing to tolerate the risk.

How can you judge what your expected rate of return will be? Again, it requires a careful study of your opponent. Many so-called loose and aggressive players with a high beta do not offer you the high expected rate of return you may think. These players are often very adept at switching speeds and avoiding traps. What may look like chaotic play on their part is really well orchestrated to help them gain chips. This is a tough style to pull off. Others may just shoot from the hip and are highly loose and aggressive without a master plan. These are the players from whom you can expect a higher rate of return. If you can withstand the risk, then it may be worth your while to take some shots at these guys.

A Look at Net Present Value

Companies must make decisions based on the net present value of money. In simple terms, you would assign a discount rate (based on some market factor) to come up with the net present value of money that you will spend or receive in the future. For instance, if you had a choice of spending between $10,000 three years from now or $5,000 now for the same piece of equipment, you would do a net present value calculation to see which makes the most sense. Where it gets tricky is that each company will need to do a calculation specific to them. For instance, say a company is faced with a choice of leasing equipment critical to their business for five years or buying the same equipment up front. The company knows that if it buys the equipment, it will take three years for it to break even (as opposed to leasing) on a net present value basis. In the remaining two years, the company will make money. Seems like an easy choice to buy, right? The answer is that it depends. For a well-established, cash-rich company, it will be an easy choice to buy. For a cash-poor start-up company that may not even be around three years from now, the answer is probably not to buy. It would be better off leasing since it needs the cash up front.

How is this relevant to a poker tournament? Let's look at a poker tournament that starts with one hundred people, and each person begins with $1,000 in chips. By the time half the people are eliminated, the average chip stack will be $2,000 in chips. By the time we are down to twenty-five people, the average chip stack will then be $4,000. So $1,000 at the beginning of a tournament is the equivalent of $4,000 when we are down to twenty-five people, right? Not necessarily. Tournaments are structured so that the blinds and antes increase at regular intervals. As a tournament progresses, luck often becomes a bigger part of the game at later levels. In addition, at the beginning of a poker tournament everyone has $1,000. At the later stages, $4,000 will be an average, but many players will have far greater than this amount. The advantages of a large stack increase the deeper you are into a tournament.

So, in actuality, that $4,000 at twenty-five people is really less powerful than the $1,000 at the beginning of a tournament. Common wisdom is that if you can maintain an average stack, you're progressing nicely. In truth, you need to be maintaining a larger than average stack as the tournament progresses if you're going to win. The further you get into a tournament, the greater percentage above average you want to be. Don't ever be satisfied with an average stack. While it's not time to panic, it's time to be creative and accumulate chips.

Know Your Burn Rate

Playing a tournament is akin to starting up a business. New businesses must manage their cash carefully. The burn rate of a start-up business is the amount of time it will take to eat up all its remaining cash. For example, if a company had $2,000,000 in cash and burns through approximately $250,000 each month to operate, then that company would be out of money in eight months unless it could find a way to save or acquire more money.

When you are playing a tournament, you have a burn rate. If you have $5,000 in chips and each round will cost you $500 in blinds and antes, then you can last ten more rounds unless you find a way to save or acquire chips. Since you are required to post blinds and antes, you must acquire more chips before you run out. The time to start thinking about acquiring chips is always sooner than later. Just like a business will have an easier time acquiring financing when it has some cash on hand, a poker player will find it easier to acquire chips when he has some chips on hand. Those chips are his source to raise funds.

Use those chips wisely. Don't squander them. Every time you waste chips, your burn rate increases and the amount of time until you go bust shortens. Think about that the next time you're tempted to call a bet on a whim or a draw.

Gambling vs. Expected Value

A lot of poker literature is written in absolutes. You will see a lot of poker authors who rely heavily on mathematics and turn each hand into an EV equation, that is, if you have positive EV, then you make the call. If you have negative EV, you do not. To offer an example, say you flop the nut flush draw. You are confident that if you hit the flush draw, you will win, but if you do not hit the flush draw, you will lose. Since you have about a 35 percent chance of winning, if the pot is offering you more than 3–1 on your money, you should call. If the pot is not, then you should fold.

Now this is a simple example and is not totally accurate. You would also have to weigh the fact that you may face another bet on the turn and, conversely, the fact that you may be able to win more money if you do hit the flush. However, to illustrate the point, I have made this a rather simple example. Now I am not going to argue that EV is not a critical component of any poker player's analysis. I am going to argue, however, that it is not the sole criteria—especially in tournament poker.

As mentioned earlier, you have to consider, among many other things, the number of chips you will be left with, the level of the blinds, the skill level of your opponents, and the knowledge of how far away from (or into) the money you are. Even if you are at the end of the game and looking to cut a deal, EV is not the absolute be all and end all.

I think a good way of looking at this is to use the game show *Deal or No Deal* as an example. For those not familiar with the show, each contestant picks one case out of about thirty cases. Each case contains a dollar amount of money from $1 to $1,000,000. The contestant's case is opened last. The contestant then starts picking other cases to be opened. As each case is opened, the EV of the contestant's case will go up or down depending on what is revealed. For instance, if fifteen cases can be eliminated and most of them are in the $1–$10,000 range, leaving cases such as the $1,000,000 case still in play, then the greater the chance that the contestant holds a case with big money. As well, a banker is on the sidelines who is willing to pay the contestant for her case depending on the perceived EV. The banker will make offers at selected intervals, but the EV at the beginning will not be a lot since there are so many cases left. However, if the contestant is fortunate enough to eliminate most of the smaller cases, his or her EV will go up dramatically and so will the bid from the banker.

Let's look at a few examples to see how relevant the EV is. Say you're a contestant on the show, and after you pick your case, your EV is $10,000. The banker offers you $20,000. From an EV point of view, this is a fantastic offer. Yet, I would bet that 99 percent of us would reject the offer. Why? Because we want to take a chance at some big money. How often do you get that chance on a game show? The $20,000 isn't going to make much of a difference in your lifestyle. We're willing to gamble a little bit here because there's some huge potential upside.

Now let's say you are down to the final two cases. There is a case of $1 and a case of $1,000,000. Your EV is approximately $500,000. The banker offers you $450,000. I would be willing to bet that the great majority of us would accept the banker's deal, even though it is a negative EV deal. Why? Because $500,000 is a lot of money that can make a big difference in most of our lives. More important, most of us are not willing to risk going home with $1 at this point when we can be guaranteed $450,000. We don't like to gamble that much.

No matter what the EV is in poker, there is a lot of luck involved. That is why you have certain stages of the tournament when it makes sense to gamble and certain times that it does not. If you are getting close to the big money, why take a chance in getting busted out just because you have a positive EV to call? Conversely, if you have a huge stack and have the opportunity to eliminate a short stack (even though it is a negative EV play) and move up in the money, it may be worth doing. If it is time for a deal and you can get some guaranteed big money at a slightly negative EV, do not completely rule it out if that money is meaningful. Anything can happen in poker.

In many of these examples, you can even argue that EV is a fluid concept and not absolute. For instance, what are the odds that you will be on a game show like *Deal or No Deal*? If you factor that in, then that original $20,000 positive EV that we would all reject may in fact be a negative EV after all.

What are the odds that you'll make the final table of the World Series of Poker main event? No matter how good you are, the odds are probably fairly long. So at that point, who's to say what the EV is for certain hands or cutting a deal?

Negotiating the Table

When I was working on Wall Street, we would do everything we could to control the negotiating process. We would want to be the party drafting the documents, we would want to have the negotiating sessions in our office, and we would want to lead the discussions. Now the parties we were negotiating against were typically very sophisticated. They were just not going to roll over for us. The edge we would get from controlling the negotiations ranged from very slight to moderate depending on the experience and skill level of the other side. In negotiating contracts in deals worth hundreds of millions of dollars, any edge you can get, you take. Even a slight edge may save your client a significant amount of money or liability.

How do you control the negotiations at the poker table? Only one thing speaks at the table, and that's your chips. You control the table by betting or raising. To do that, you have to be selective about the hands you enter into, and when you do enter into, you should be taking the lead in the betting. This puts the pressure on your opponent. Think how you feel when someone bets into you or raises your bet. Unless you have the nuts, it's the added pressure on you that forces you to make tough decisions. When you force your opponent into tough decisions, you find out more information. So by taking the lead in the betting and controlling the negotiations at the table, you may be able to force your opponent out of the hand or find out how strong your opponent really is.

Let me give you another reason why position is so important in Hold'em. Late position is akin to controlling the documents in drafting and holding the negotiations in the home office. This is where you can control the process. You are sitting in the leader's chair so lead and don't follow.

In poker, every edge you can get is important. Just like in negotiating, when you control the betting at the table, your edge will depend on the skill and experience of your opponents. That edge will range from small to fairly significant because there are plenty of opponents out there who are easily controlled.

A Lesson from Cash Games

If you are a cash game player, you should already know about game selection. In short, you choose a game that you expect to be profitable for you. You find opponents you can exploit and a money level at which you are comfortable playing. If possible, you even try to choose your specific seat in order to have position on certain players.

When playing a tournament, you have no say on what table or seat you occupy. You have no control on when that table will be broken up or when and where you will be moved. Therefore, most players give little or no thought to game selection when choosing a tournament. That's not smart poker.

First, you should always choose a tournament at a buy-in that is affordable to you. If you want to play a bigger tournament than you can afford, then play a satellite and try to win your buy-in. The reason this is so important is that it will affect your play. If you enter a tournament for the experience, you cannot win. You will be trying to get your money's worth by surviving for as long as possible instead of trying to win the thing. How do you know if a tournament is affordable? Ask yourself one simple question before you enter: Am I willing to risk my entire stack on the first hand if the situation dictates that that is the correct thing to do? If your answer is anything other than an emphatic yes, find a lower buy-in tournament.

Next, even though you cannot pick which opponents will sit at your table, you can select tournaments based on the overall competitiveness of the field. Even if you can afford a tournament, try to find one that will be profitable for you. Pick a structure that suits your game.

I was in Vegas a few years back with a friend of mine who had never played tournament poker before, so we picked a low buy-in tournament at the Luxor for him to test the waters. It was only a $20 buy-in, and we started with about fifty players. Before the tournament started, I asked for a sheet of the blind structure and was informed that they did not have one. The person at the desk did not know what the blinds would be. Since they held these tournaments every day, I asked how long they usually lasted. She told me that they were generally done in less than two hours.

I thought for sure she was mistaken because I could not fathom how a fifty-person tournament could move so quickly. I soon found out how wrong I was. We started with $250 in chips with blinds at $10–$25 and with blinds that doubled every ten minutes. It was basically a game of roulette masquerading as a poker tournament. Luck was at a premium and skill was rendered irrelevant. I managed to survive about halfway through the field before making my exit. The only reason I even managed to last is that everyone was scared to death of being the first one eliminated. There was this house custom to announce publicly the name of the first person eliminated and nobody wanted that embarrassment. Personally, I could not care less, and I used that time to pick up some chips. It did not take long, however, for the first elimination and then it was all potluck Hold'em.

As luck would have it, my friend came in fifth place. As bad as this tournament was for me, it was ideal for him. It was a great introduction to tournament poker because he got the full experience (albeit in a very condensed form) of playing in a tournament and lasting to the final table.

A tournament like this will never be profitable for me no matter how bad the competition is. In choosing a tournament, make sure to consider both the level of competition and the blind structure. Then go play to win!

Tells

In Mike Caro's seminal work on the topic of tells, *Caro's Book of Poker Tells*, he discusses how one of the biggest tells inexperienced players make is to act weak when they are strong and to act strong when they are weak. I had a recent experience that illustrates the point. In fact, this player was so obvious that it was laughable. We were playing a one-table sit and go at the Trump Taj Mahal. It was a ten-person $100 + $20 entry fee with the winner taking the entire $1,000 prize pool.

With about five players left, I was in the big blind with A-6. A player in late position limped in as did the small blind. I checked and we saw the flop three handed. The flop came A-K-K. The small blind checked and I bet out. The player in late position folded, and the small blind smooth called. Because this player had been playing tight, his move put me on notice. The turn brought a 7 and now the small blind bet out, making a rather substantial bet. At this point, I was still not sure if he had the King or an ace. If he did have an ace, he could easily have me outkicked. As I was contemplating what to do, my opponent said to the rest of the table, "Uh-oh, I think I am in trouble." Of course, he was trying to pretend he had a weak hand. That was his first mistake. He was being so obvious, though, that I actually thought he might very well be weak and was trying to act like he was strong by being so obvious about being weak.

I did not think this guy was that clever, though, and I folded my hand. He then turned over his King to remove all doubt. That was his second mistake. Well, as luck would have it, the tournament came down to the two of us heads-up. I had a slight chip advantage when the following hand came up. I limped in from the small blind with J♥-4♥. He checked from the big blind. The flop came 9♠-4♣-2♥. He checked and I made a pot-sized bet with my middle pair. He called. The turn brought the A♥ and he moved all-in. Now I was fairly certain he did not have an ace or he would have raised pre-flop with it. I was also fairly certain he did not have a nine or he would have bet the flop. I was somewhat sure that I had the best hand. Even if I did not, I had a flush draw. My thought process was largely irrelevant, though, because my opponent was staring me down about six inches from my face. I had to swallow so hard to avoid laughing. I mean this guy was too funny. If he hadn't shown that King before, I very well might have folded thinking this guy was trying some kind of reverse psychology. As it was, I knew I had him beat. I called, and sure enough he turned over K-2 for bottom pair. The river brought no help and I won the tournament.

In my book *Tournament Poker and The Art of War*, I quote a couple of Sun Tzu's passages that discuss feigning weakness when strong and projecting strength when weak. I believe those concepts are integral to success at no-limit Texas Hold'em tournaments. How then can you implement those concepts without giving off an obvious tell as Mike Caro suggests?

First thing to remember is not to act or oversell your weakness or strength. Don't do what my opponent in the previous hand did. That's a dead giveaway of the sort Mike Caro so acutely observes. If you find yourself wanting to "act" a certain way, think of the previous example and stop yourself. So now that we know how not to do it, let's look at how to do it. The primary way to feign weakness or project strength is through your betting. For example, say you're in the big blind with J-7 off-suit. You get two limpers in front of you so that you have a free look at the flop. The flop comes 2-3-8 rainbow. This is the type of flop that is unlikely to have helped anyone. Since you could have anything in the big blind, you can make a move for this pot. Of course, your opponents may suspect you of making a move. So if you come out firing and forcibly throw your chips in the pot, you may give yourself away. Instead of doing that, why not try a check-raise bluff? Check the flop and wait for someone to bet at it. When he does, raise him. This serves two purposes: First, you're much more likely to be believed. A check-raise projects strength. Next, you'll win a bigger pot.

If you want to project strength, then pretend that you have a strong hand. Go back to the preceding example and play that hand like you have pocket threes and you hit middle set. That's how you project strength. Conversely, if you did actually have pocket threes, then play the hand as if you had 4-5 off-suit and were drawing to the straight.

When trying to pick up tells from others, some will be as obvious as my clueless opponent's just were, but the great majority won't. Take the time to study each opponent, though, and you'll be surprised by how much information you can pick up. Instead of looking for facial tics, study their betting patterns to pick up tendencies. That information is likely to be more useful.

Picking up physical tells is not like in the movies. In the great majority of cases, you are not going to see a noticeable physical trait like an opponent always rubbing his nose when he is bluffing. Instead, I try to size up my opponent. Is he the type to try to "act" like my opponent in the first example in this chapter. If so, how good is he at acting? Does he know that I have picked up on his acting, and will he try a reverse tell? If an opponent is not acting, then what is he doing? Does he do the same thing every single time? Does he genuinely take his time when he is truly conflicted? Will he change gears and try to sell a tell if he thinks I have picked up on his habits?

So many subtleties can be found in just one opponent in poker. Now multiply that by nine, and you can start to understand why it is so critical to study your opponents at the table. Do not take a hand off. Even if you fold, stay attuned to the action so you can pick up on who is doing what and how. It may seem tedious, but what else do you have to do? I promise that it will pay off.

Put Yourself in the Mind of Your Opponent

There are a lot of familiar plays and universal strategies in poker. Yet each player has his own unique individual style of play. It is human nature to project our own way of thinking onto others. This is a big mistake in any aspect of life. If you project your way of thinking onto your opponent at the poker table, it can cost you money. Rather, you should be studying your opponents and trying to get inside their heads. Think how they play. If you are not in a hand, you should still be focusing on the action. In fact, I find that I can pick up more on a player when I am not in a hand. I can totally focus on my opponent's actions and try to guess exactly what he is doing and why.

Once you pick up a few things, it can pay off in a big way. Let me offer an example from an event at the U.S. Poker Championships. The blinds were $100–$200 and I had about $4,500 in chips, which was about an average stack at the time. I was under the gun with A♠-K♠ and raised to make it $600 to go. Both the small and big blind called so that I would have position throughout the hand. The flop came 8♣-9♥-4♥. This was a horrible flop for me. These cards were of no use to me and very easily could have helped the blinds. I still had position at least. Both blinds checked the flop, and I bet $1,500, which I thought was enough to chase these guys out without committing myself to the pot. To my surprise, both players called. I put at least one of them on a draw, but I was also worried that one of them might have top pair and that he was not going to let go.

The turn brought more bad news with the 9♠. Now I was worried that someone just made trips. Even if they thought I had an overpair, they had to know they had the best hand now. Both players checked, and being worried about a trap, I decided to check as well. Both players looked relieved. The river brought the 2♦.

Seeing this card, the small blind moved all-in. The big blind quickly folded. Now I had seen the small blind make some moves for pots before when he sensed no one had hit. The big blind had been more of a calling station willing to call for draws and fold when he missed. Now the small blind had me covered, and it would cost me all my chips to see if he was bluffing. If he missed his straight or flush draw, my ace high was probably the best hand. Although there was a chance he had a hand like A-8 suited. However, something about the way he committed his chips reminded me of a previous play he had made, and I decided to call. He turned over J♥-10♥. He had missed both a flush and an open-ended straight draw. He had also read me correctly that I didn't have anything. What he had not counted on was my calling with nothing but ace high. The rest of the table looked shocked that I had called and scooped a big pot.

Now I don't recommend doing this quite often. Unless you really have a great read on your opponent, it's never wise to call off all your chips with nothing but ace high. In fact, in hindsight I don't think I played this hand very well. I think I should've bet the turn.

However, the larger point here is that you can win a lot of pots by getting inside the mind of your opponent. One of my favorite things to watch for is a player who likes to fire three bullets at the pot when he has completely missed. Now, this is a good way to play against most opponents. If you raise pre-flop, you should continue to be aggressive post-flop. There's a common poker adage that an amateur will fire one bullet at the pot while a pro will fire two or three. In the previous example, where I raised pre-flop, I fired one bullet after I completely missed the flop. Yet, I didn't bet the turn and failed to fire the proverbial second bullet.

When I know my opponent will fire those extra bullets, I'll let him bluff off his chips to me. For example, I was playing another event at the U.S. Poker Championships when I was looking to trap a very aggressive opponent. He raised from late position, and I called from the big blind holding J♣-9♣. The flop came Q♣-J♦-3♠. I checked and he made a big bet. I called. The turn brought the 4♣. Again, I checked. I was still fairly certain my hand was the best and that my opponent would try to bully me off it. He made another very big bet on the turn. Again, I called. The river brought the best possible card for me—the A♣. I had the second nuts. I was also hoping my opponent had an ace. I checked and my opponent went all-in. I quickly called, and he reluctantly turned over his A-3 for two pair. He made some comment about how lucky I was and when was he going to learn not to bet against players who don't know better than to fold.

Of course, I did get lucky on the river. But the fact remains that I had the better hand the entire way after the flop. I knew I had the best hand, and I let my opponent bluff off his chips to me. Usually I am not a big fan of slow playing, and it was extremely risky to slow play a hand as vulnerable as mine was even if I thought I had the best hand. If I had bet or raised anywhere along the way, I could have helped define my opponent's hand. In this case, though, I really did not think I needed to do that. I knew enough about my opponent to know how he played that I thought the best way to maximize my profits here was for him to bet the hand for me.

It's amazing how many times I see similar plays (either from others or from myself), and the reaction of the aggressive player is always one of indignation that he can't believe the winner of the hand could call. Now in some of these cases, I do think some players are just calling stations, and they're calling with marginal hands and praying that they have the best hand rather than having a good read on their opponents. However, I know for certain that many of these so-called weaker opponents are completely exploiting their overly aggressive opponents to maximize their profits.

I find the arrogance of the aggressive player when he is called down and caught bluffing to be very telling. I see it with some top pros up against so-called amateurs all the time. These players believe that they are entitled to the pot for their so-called correct aggressive play and that their opponents are too dumb for their own good. While that may be the case at times, I think many of these so-called amateurs are craftier than they are given credit for.

Understand and Evaluate Your Opponent's Options

In any negotiations, I always make it a point to know and understand the other side's options completely. Let's look at an example that almost all of us can relate to—buying a house. If you are buying a house in a resale, you should know what options the seller has. Are there other potential buyers? Is the seller in a hurry to sell? Well, if the house has been on the market for a while, you are the only potential buyer, and the seller has already moved out, then you should be able to make any reasonable offer. In addition, you should be able to take a firm stance after the home inspection. Now that the seller has accepted your offer, he will want to salvage the deal. He does not want to lose the only buyer he has been able to get to sign a contract. Furthermore, depending on the nature of the problems revealed by the inspection, the seller may now have to disclose those problems to any other potential buyers up front. The seller is now very involved in the hand. He is pot committed at this point.

The further along you are in any deal, the harder it will be for either party to walk away. People do not want to have to start over again. Recognizing this should help you use this to your advantage. Now how does this relate to poker?

In no-limit tournaments, you want to know how much an opponent is willing to invest in a hand and how easily he will fold. If you are going to be the aggressor, your opponent has three options: fold, call, or raise. In order to maximize your profits, you have to have a fairly good understanding of how likely each of those options is for the particular opponent in that specific hand. For instance, if you are able to see a free flop from the big blind with 8-9 off-suit and the flop comes 5-6-7 rainbow, your goal at this point is to win as much money as possible. Thus, you want to limit the fold option of your opponent. Maybe you make a small value bet to increase the pot and give your opponent more incentive to play on. Maybe you check in the hopes that your opponent's hand improves on the turn. The further along and more involved a player is in a hand, the harder it is for him to fold.

If you are looking to force your opponent to fold, again understand his options. It is pointless to try to steal the blinds and antes when the big blind is so short stacked that he is going to call without even looking at his cards. No matter what the situation, evaluate and understand your opponent's options before declaring your course of action.

The Mental Challenge

Poker tournaments can require a tremendous amount of endurance. Major events can last for up to six days. With the increasing number of entries, even one day events can take up to twenty hours to play. In no-limit play, when one mistake can mean elimination, maintaining the right frame of mind and staying focused is perhaps your biggest challenge at the poker table.

Personally, I know I've played well in tournaments for two straight days, only to suffer a brain freeze and make one foolish mistake that sends me to the rail just out of the money. I see it happen just about every tournament. Players get tired or hungry or grow impatient and lose their focus and discipline. Let's look at how you can stay mentally fresh throughout the tournament.

Come Prepared

While you have no control over how long a tournament will last or how frequently you will be given breaks, you do have control over how fresh you are at the begining of the event. Get a good night's sleep and eat a decent meal before the tournament begins. Get some quiet time in and get in the right frame of mind. Make a mental checklist of those things you want to accomplish. If you have been playing too loose lately, remind yourself to tighten up. If you have been playing a lot of cash games, then put yourself in a tournament frame of mind. If it helps, write down some notes and put them in your pocket. Make sure you are dressed comfortably. Casinos can be very cold, even if it is hot outside. You may want to bring a sweatshirt or light jacket with you that you can slip on or off.

To the extent possible, sign up ahead of time so that you can avoid any lines or even the possibility that the tournament sells out. Get a copy of the tournament structure so that you know how fast the blinds will increase in relation to the starting chip stack amounts. Know how patient you can afford to be before the blinds will start eating you up. Study when the breaks will occur and plan your meals accordingly. Ask if you will be receiving a meal voucher and, if so, where you can use it. Know what restaurants are crowded and which ones allow you to get a quick bite to eat. When you get a break, you want to make sure you get away from the table and reflect without being rushed.

Check out your starting table and, if need be, adjust the seat distances. I find that the seats are never left a uniform distance apart. Often one side is more crowded than the other is. That is why I like to get to the table first and spread the seats out so that I am not boxed in. Anticipate what you will need during the tournament and bring a bottle of water or a snack with you. If you pack a snack, make sure it can be eaten quickly and with minimum distraction.

Stay Focused

Staying focused is easy at the beginning of a tournament. Players are accustomed to being patient and studying their opponents. As the tournament progresses, it is quite easy to lose focus. New players come to your table, and you may not be able to study them as thoroughly as you should. You find your eyes wandering when you are not in the hand. The guy next to you may be overly chatty and distract you. You may be thirsty and find yourself focused on waving over a cocktail waitress. You may not be able to get a previous hand out of your mind.

If you find yourself losing focus, make little tests for yourself. Before each hand, pick one player to study. If he folds, pick someone else. Or try to guess what cards each player is holding or what move he is likely to make. If you fold your cards, still play along with the hand. Determine what you think would be the best strategy for the players involved considering their positions. In short, do whatever you need to do to stay focused. Every time the dealer shuffles the cards, take that as a cue to sharpen your focus and get involved.

In the later stages of a tournament, I find one sure tell sign whether a player is maintaining his focus. Invariably, someone will forget to put in his ante. That player who forgets on more than one occasion does not have the right focus. If you forget even once, take that as a wake-up call to get your head in the game. Many times when the pot is short an ante, no one is quite sure who did not put in his ante. The player who is really focused will not only put his ante in, but he will know exactly who else has and who has not.

Poker Etiquette

With the exploding popularity of poker, proper etiquette is sometimes sorely lacking at the table. This has prompted a number of casinos to enact new rules that are strictly enforced. Make sure you know these rules ahead of time so you can avoid penalties. The number one rule that is gaining widespread acceptance is the F-bomb rule. Say the F-word (or any derivation thereof) and you get an automatic ten-minute penalty. Many players have argued that the rule is unfair in that you can be penalized for an innocent muttering of the word under your breath not directed toward anyone. Conversely, you can berate an opponent without using the F-word and not face any penalty. Certainly, there is a kind of injustice there.

However, poker is a game of discipline. If you do not have the discipline to control your language at the table, your game can probably use a ten-minute break. Anyway, the rule is about as cut and dried as a rule can be, so no one should have any reason to complain. Some other rules or matters of etiquette are not as cut and dried and require a little discussion.

Don't Discuss a Hand When There Is Still Action

If there is still action at the table, do not discuss the hand. As a rule, I would avoid discussing a hand altogether unless you are trying to gather information. Too many times when you discuss a hand, you are giving away information. Regardless of your intentions, it is a clear no-no to discuss a hand until all the action has stopped. It is not fair to the players in the pot.

For instance, one thing I see all the time is a flop come say 9-9-2 and a player not in the hand will grimace and tell his neighbor that he folded a 9. While this seems like an innocent comment, it is anything but. If the players involved in the pot know that one of the other 9's is dead, that is critical information to their evaluation of the hand and unfair exposure of what their opponent could possibly hold. Even if you do not get penalized for making this kind of statement, you are sure to hear from one of the other players, and that is a distraction you can do without.

That's another reason to avoid discussing hands in general—even after the action is over. If you offer your opinion, not only do you give away information, but you risk getting into a heated exchange with another player. Your goal is to maintain your focus and not create more distractions for yourself.

The Right to Know Your Opponent's Cards

In just about any form of poker, if a player stays until the very end of a hand, everyone else at the table has a right to see his cards. That's right. If you call a bet on the river and watch your opponent turn over the winning hand, anyone else at the table can ask to see your cards before you muck them. Here's a situation where rules and etiquette collide. As a practical matter, you'll hardly ever see a player ask to see another's hand if he wants to muck. It's poor etiquette and it's also poor poker. As useful as that information may be, I would caution in asking for it. You may incur the wrath of the entire table and, again, you don't need additional distractions. You're also likely to be asked to turn over your cards the next time you want to muck a losing hand.

The only time I find this rule advantageous is when playing online. As mentioned earlier, if you are playing online, you cannot literally ask a player to show his cards. However, you can request hand histories from the site and you will usually receive an e-mail within seconds. That hand history will reveal the cards of everyone seeing the hand to the end whether or not they showed them to the table. So if you play a tournament online and are curious about what cards an opponent played, request a hand history. You will have your answer within seconds, and your opponents will never know that you requested the information. There is nothing unethical about this at all, but be aware that your opponents may be getting the same information on you.

Don't Act Out of Turn

This is another rule that seems like common sense from both a poker point of view and an ethical point of view. Since poker is a game of imperfect information, position becomes all-important. If you are in late position, you have the advantage of seeing how everyone else acts before you do so. If you act out of turn, you give up that advantage. Even if you are planning to fold, everyone may fold to you, and you may have an opportunity to pick up a pot. Folding out of turn can also hurt or help some of your opponents and serve to irritate them. For instance, if the player before you has mixed feelings about what to do and he witnesses you folding before he has made up his mind, he may now be more likely to call or raise. While acting out of turn typically does not carry a penalty, it is an important rule to follow. If you are acting out of turn, it is a clear sign that your focus needs some fine-tuning.

One way to avoid acting out of turn pre-flop is to wait until it is your turn to look at your cards. This is a good practice to get into for a number of reasons: First, your attention can be focused on studying your opponents rather than looking at your cards. Next, you will avoid making up your mind as to what to do until it is your turn to act, which is when you will have maximum information. Last, this can also prevent you from inadvertently signaling your intentions prior to your turn to act.

Don't Bet or Raise Less Than the Minimum Amount

When playing no limit with increasing blinds, it is easy to get distracted as to the proper minimum betting limits. Just remember that the minimum opening bet on every street is always equal to the amount of the big blind, and that any raise must at least equal the previous raise. For instance, if the blinds are $100–$200, then regardless of how the betting went pre-flop, the first person who wants to bet post-flop must bet at least $200. Of course, they can bet any amount higher up to their entire stack, and there is no rule as to what increments they bet in. So now, say someone opens the post-flop betting round by betting $325. If you want to raise, you have to raise at least $325 more for a total of $650. Of course, you can raise any amount greater than that as well.

Once you say raise, you are committed to raising the minimum amount even if you mistakenly thought that you could raise a lesser amount.

Sprezzatura

Baldassare Castiglione was a sixteenth-century Italian humanist, diplomat, and author. His most famous work is *The Book of the Courtier* in which he advocates that one should preserve one's composure and self-control under all circumstances. He also preached the practice of *sprezzatura*, which loosely translated means to conduct all things in a nonchalant manner that conceals all artistry and makes one's actions seem uncontrolled and effortless.

While this seems like sound advice for most of life's pursuits, it is dead on for one's behavior at the poker table. First, you should always maintain your composure and self-control at the poker table. That means more than not going on tilt. It means having patience and discipline and the ability to stay focused on everything happening at the table so that you are ready to exploit any opportunity while minimizing your mistakes.

The second part of Castiglione's advice is more interesting. How do you benefit from behaving in a nonchalant manner and making your actions appear effortless? I think you benefit in a number of ways: First, maintaining a nonchalant persona will help you preserve your composure and self-control. Next, it will make your actions incredibly difficult to read. How will your opponents be able to put you on a hand if every time you act, you project a smooth and controlled image? Finally, your seemingly effortless moves are likely to affect your opponent's play. They may relax too much and let their guard down. Once they do, they are bound to make mistakes. Little do they know that beneath the nonchalant surface you are projecting is a monster poker player exerting a great deal of effort.

The key to sprezzatura is the appearance of effortless mastery. Don't forget that. To practice sprezzatura is to take on a bigger workload. Not only are you doing all the things you should be doing at the poker table, but now you have to work that much harder to make it appear effortless. Next time you are watching poker on television, try to disregard the hole cards and study each player to see who has mastered the art of sprezzatura. I think you will find that many of the top players possess that uncanny ability and use it to their advantage.

The Best of the Blog

I often draw comparisons between poker and other areas of life. As I have mentioned previously, I think that poker principles have enormous applications in other arenas and vice versa. I wrote a short series of entries called poker and politics in my blog (hosted by holdemradio.com) for which I received a tremendous amount of positive feedback and discussion. I thought I would include some of those entries here for a couple of reasons: First, I hope you will gain some insight that will help your poker game. Next, and more important, I hope you will get to view other arenas in a more critical way so that you can start drawing your own poker analogies every day to help your game.

Poker is a game of never-ending learning. Since we can't play poker twenty-four hours a day (and even if we could, I'm not sure how beneficial it would be), I think it's extremely helpful to be well rounded and learn to recognize and incorporate poker strategies from things we experience, witness, or read about every day. With that in mind, I hope that you enjoy this chapter and that you find plenty of useful analogies from your own experiences.

Poker and Politics, Part I

This may seem like an odd title and I promise not to make this blog a partisan one. After all, poker is a great equalizer for all of us regardless of age, size, sex, and political affiliation. I do, however, think that there are some lessons to be learned from politics that can help your poker game. So here goes the first of a few blogs that'll cover that topic.

Let's go back to November 2004 when George W. Bush won the election in a close race against John Kerry. What was the biggest reason for his success? To me, I think it was clear that Bush ran a more effective campaign. And by effective, I mean his campaign took a focused take-no-prisoners approach. It was Machiavellian. Led by Rove and others, this was clearly a group that understood how to obtain and maintain power. Kerry's campaign on the other hand was unfocused and directionless. The turning point for me was when Kerry was attacked on his Vietnam service and did nothing to defend himself. Even voters who were appalled by the attack on Kerry were shocked that Kerry did not fight back. How could this guy defend us against terrorism when he can't even defend himself from arguably baseless attacks? Regardless of which side better represents your viewpoint, Bush's campaign clearly ran the more Machiavellian one.

Now you can argue that campaigns should be devoid of Machiavellian tactics, and while that's idealistic, it has never been the case. What no one can argue, however, is that the poker room is one arena in which you can exercise true Machiavellian tactics. Making that transition from your civilian self to the ruthless poker player (who maintains an air of civility to his opponents) is a tough one. Power at the poker table equals profit. Next time you sit down at the felt, concentrate on ruling the table, and you'll find the chips coming your way soon enough. Play to Win!

Poker and Politics, Part II

Okay, I am going to talk about the Iraq war, but again this is meant to be nonpartisan. The fact is that no matter how you feel about the war, it has become a political football. Bush's approval ratings are at record lows and the majority of Americans now question why we went into Iraq in the first place. You would think then that the Democrats would have a golden opportunity to gain some political points. However, the Democrats' approval ratings are no better than the Republicans are.

Without getting into the merits of whether it was worthwhile going to Iraq, let's look at how the Democrats have bumbled this opportunity. If you're going to attack an opponent, go after their vulnerable points. The Democrats in this case keep talking about the lack of weapons of mass destruction. Well, at the time of the invasion, everyone thought Saddam had them, and in any event, he was blatantly disregarding UN resolutions and inspections. If you recall, though, the justification for going into Iraq was this so-called connection between Saddam and Osama Bin Laden that never existed. At the time of the invasion of Iraq, over half the Americans believed that Saddam was responsible for 9/11. This is the point that the Democrats should be hammering home. This is where Republicans are most vulnerable.

Next time you are playing poker, try to identify your opponent's weak points. Maybe he raises a lot but backs down to a re-raise. Maybe he is strong pre-flop but will back down post-flop. Maybe he plays position well but does not like to play anything out of position. The point is, by all means attack his weak spots. And to do that, you have to first identify what they are. As simple as that sounds, many poker players ignore weak spots and instead attack what is convenient—just like the Democrats in my example.

Poker and Politics, Part III

Since my last entry, I have noticed that President Bush's approval ratings, while still low, have made a significant leap up. Of course, the elections in Iraq have had something to do with that. More important, in my opinion, have been the President's own speeches. For most of his presidency, Bush has been criticized for being unable to admit mistakes, and previously Bush has not wavered in the face of such criticism. Since he won reelection last year, it's hard to argue with his previous stance. However, lately Bush has been admitting faults and shortcomings in connection with the war. He has even reached out to some critics of the war instead of questioning their patriotism. In short, Bush has switched gears in order to re-establish his image.

What can we learn from this? At the poker table, you cannot be so rigid as to become too predictable. While it is important to study your opponents, it is just as important to know what your opponents think of you.

You have to be aware of your table image at all times and know when it is time for an adjustment. If opponents are starting to pick on you, you must fight back. If you have been bullying the table and players are starting to raise you, it is time to tighten up. Poker is a fluid game, so stay aware of your surroundings. Good luck and play to win.

Glossary

Ace rag: In Hold'em, to have an ace and a card below a ten. Also referred to as Ax.

All-in: To place all of one's chips in the pot. To go all-in is to bet your entire stack.

Angle shooting: An unethical move short of cheating designed to give you and edge.

Ante: A set amount of chips that each player (including the blinds) must place in the pot before a hand is dealt. In no-limit Hold'em tournaments, antes typically are not required until the later rounds.

Bad beat: Having a strong hand beaten by an opponent who was a big underdog but makes a lucky draw. This is especially true when your opponent is playing poorly, and he should not have been in the pot in the first place.

Bet: To be the first to place chips into the pot on any given round.

Big blind: Typically, the position that is two spots to the left of the button. The big blind must lead the first round of betting with a forced full bet.

Big stack: Having more chips than the great majority of players at your table.

Blank: A card that does not help any player.

Blind: A forced bet that one or two players are forced to make to start the first round of betting. The blinds will be the first to act in each subsequent round of betting, and, thus, to be in the blind is to be in an unfavorable position. The blinds rotate around the table with each deal and are always to the left of the button.

Blinded out: To lose your chip stack as a result of posting the mandatory blinds and antes.

Bluff: A bet or raise made to force your opponent to fold when you sense he is vulnerable even though he may have a better hand.

Board: The five community cards placed in the center of the table.

Bubble: See "on the bubble."

Button: A disk that rotates around the table with each new deal. The player on the button acts last during each round of betting. Thus, to be on the button is to be in the most favorable position.

Call: To place into the pot an amount of chips equal to an opponent's bet or raise.

Caller: A player who makes a call.

Calling station: A weak player who will call just about any bet but will rarely bet or raise. This type of player is extremely hard to bluff.

Chase: To stay in a hand with hopes of outdrawing an opponent with a superior hand.

Check: To pass when it is your turn to bet.

Check-raise: To check and then raise after your opponent bets.

Chip: A round token used to represent varying denominations of money.

Come over the top: To raise or re-raise with a huge bet.

Covered: To have someone covered means you have more chips than he does.

Cutoff: That position that is to the immediate right of the button and acts right before the button.

Drawing dead: Holding a hand that cannot possibly win because no matter what card comes up, your opponent will still hold a superior hand.

Draw out: To improve your hand so that it beats a previously superior hand.

Early position: Any position in which you will act before most of the other players in a round of betting. In a ten-handed game, the first five positions to the left of the button will be considered early positions.

Favorite: A hand that has the best chance of winning at any point in time before all the cards are dealt.

Fifth Street: The fifth and final community card in Hold'em. Also called the river.

Flop: The first three community cards that are all dealt at the same time.

Flush: Five cards of the same suit.

Fold: To drop out of a hand rather than call a bet or raise.

Fold equity: When you bet or raise, you increase your chances of winning since your opponents may fold. That increased opportunity to win is referred to as your fold equity.

Fourth Street: The fourth community card in Hold'em. Also called the turn.

Free card: A card that a player gets to see without having to pay for it. When no one bets on a particular round of playing, the next card is considered a free card.

Full house: Three cards of one rank and two of another such as K♦-K♠-K♣-3♠-3♦.

Gut shot: An inside straight draw.

Heads-up: To play against a single opponent.

Inside straight draw: A straight that can be completed only by a card of one rank. For example, three-four-five-seven can only be completed with a six.

In the money: In tournament play, only the top finishers will receive prize money. A player who advances to receive prize money is said to have finished in the money.

Kicker: A side card that is not part of any made hand.

Late position: Any position in which you will act after most of the other players in a round of betting. In a ten-handed game, the button and the two positions to the right of the button will be considered late positions.

Lay down: To fold your hand in the face of a bet.

Levels: Predetermined intervals of play whereby the blinds (and antes, if applicable) will be set for a period of time. The blinds will increase with each level.

Limp in: To call a bet rather than raise prior to the flop.

Loose: A player who is playing loose is playing more hands than he should.

Middle pair: To pair the second highest card on the board.

Middle position: A position in a round of betting somewhere in the middle. In a ten-handed game, the fourth and fifth positions to the right of the button are considered middle positions.

Muck: To discard a hand without revealing it.

Multiway hand or pot: A hand or pot with three or more players.

Nuts: The best possible hand at that point in time.

Off-suit: Two or more cards of different suits. If you are dealt a J♦-10♠ your hand is J-10 off-suit.

On the bubble: In tournament play, when players are only a few eliminations away from being in the money. If a player is eliminated in 28th place when 27 places were paid, that player is said to have been eliminated on the bubble.

On tilt: To be playing poorly because of a lack of control of your own play.

Open-ended straight draw: Four cards to a straight, which can be completed at either end by one of two cards of two different ranks. A 7-8-9-10 is an open-ended straight draw in that either a Jack or a 6 will complete the straight.

Outs: When you do not have the best hand, but there are still more cards to come. Those are the cards that will make your hand a winning hand and are called your outs.

Overcard(s): To have a card(s) that is higher than any card on the board. If you have K♠-J♦ and the flop is Q♥-4♣-7♠, then you have one overcard.

Pair: Two cards of the same rank such as 6♣-6♥.

Pocket: The cards received face down. If you are dealt 3♣3♦, then you have a pocket pair

Pot: The collective amount of all chips bet at any point in time.

Pot odds: The ratio of the amount of chips in the pot to the size of the bet you must call.

Put someone on a hand: To determine to the best of your ability the hand your opponent is most likely to possess.

Rainbow: Two to four cards of different suits. If the flop comes 3-6-J rainbow, then all three cards are of different suits.

Raise: To bet an additional amount after an opponent makes a bet.

Raiser: A player who makes a raise.

Rebuy: A rebuy tournament allows a player to rebuy chips for a predetermined amount of time and typically only if the player has less than the original buy-in amount. For example, if a rebuy tournament costs $100 to enter and each player receives 1,000 in chips, players will be allowed to buy an additional 1,000 in chips for another $100 so long as they have less than 1,000 chips at the time of the rebuy. The rebuy option is usually only available for the first three levels of the tournament.

River: The fifth and final community card in Hold'em.

Runner: A card that helps or completes your hand when you need help and that comes on the turn or river or both. For example, you are holding J♥-10♥ and the flop is J♠-A♥-2♦. Your opponent is holding A♦-J♣. Since no one card will help you, you need two runners in order to win. If the turn is 4♥ and the river is 9♥, you will have hit two runners and made a flush to win the hand.

Semi-bluff: To bet with the intention of inducing an opponent with a superior hand to fold, but if he does not, you have a reasonable chance to improve your hand to the best hand.

Set: In Hold'em, three of a kind when you have a pocket pair and the board contains a card of the same rank.

Short stacked: Playing with a stack of chips that is much smaller than the average chip stack of the other players.

Showdown: The turning over of all remaining players' cards after the last round of betting is concluded.

Sixth street: The sixth card dealt in seven-card stud.

Slow play: To not bet or raise with a strong hand in order to trap your opponent and, ultimately, win more chips in the hand.

Smooth call: To only call a bet with the best hand instead of raising. This is done in order to hide the strength of the strong hand in hopes of winning more chips in the next betting round.

Steal: To make a big bet or raise that induces your opponent(s) to fold when you may not have the best hand.

Stone cold nuts: The absolute best possible hand.

Straight: Five cards of mixed suits in sequence. Ace can be played as a high or low card in Hold'em.

Suited: Two or more cards of the same suit.

Tell: A nuance or mannerism a player may display that gives away his hand.

Tight: Playing very conservatively or only playing strong hands.

Trap: To conceal the strength of your hand in order to induce your opponent into betting his weaker hand.

Trips: Having three cards of the same rank made by using one card from your hand and two cards from the board.

Underdog: A hand that is not the favorite to win.

Under the gun: The first player to act on the first round of betting in Hold'em. Since the blinds have forced bets, the player to the immediate left of the big blind is "under the gun."

Recommended Additional Sources

Recommended Books

Apostolico, David. *Tournament Poker and The Art of War*. Lyle Stuart, 2005. At the risk of being self-promoting, I recommend this book. Once you have the fundamentals down, you need something more to take your game to the next level. This book applies the principles of Sun Tzu's classic to teach players how to develop the proper mindset to evaluate situations and advance far in tournaments.

Caro, Mike. *Caro's Book of Poker Tells*. Cardozo, 2003. This is the definitive book on the subject. Since poker is a game of imperfect information, understanding tells is a critical part of the game.

Harrington, Dan, and Bill Robertie. *Harrington on Hold'em*. 2 vols. Two Plus Two Publishing, 2004–2005. Former world champion Dan Harrington's two-volume set is fast becoming the definitive authority on no-limit Texas Hold'em tournaments. This is not a book for beginners. But once you have some experience under your belt, pick up both volumes to learn more advanced strategies.

Lindgren, Erick. *Making the Final Table*. HarperCollins, 2005. Terrific insight from a highly successful and aggressive tournament player. This book is sure to improve your game and help you reach the final table on a more consistent basis.

Sklansky, David. *The Theory of Poker*. Two Plus Two Publishing, 1994. While not a tournament book, this is a classic book that analyzes poker principles from the general to the very specific. Many terms, phrases, and understandings that are common knowledge in poker circles today originated in this book.

Online Resources

The last few years have seen a proliferation of websites dedicated to all things poker. Do a Google search to find one you like. Personally, I look for sites that have a broad readership and an active forum for advanced discussion.

I would highly recommend two sites: First, wptfan.com has an open posting policy. While you are likely to come across a number of different topics, there are always some interesting threads discussing specific situations in no-limit Hold'em tournaments. This site has some very knowledgeable readers who are not afraid to state their opinion.

The next site I would recommend is twoplustwo.com. This site is run by the people at Two Plus Two Publishing who put out some of the best poker books. Their website has specific forums for a broad range of poker issues. There are a couple of forums dedicated just to tournament strategy, and there is always an active and lively discussion. Post a question, and you are sure to get a number of responses.

Of course, as with anything online, be prepared for honest and sometimes harsh advice. Poker players are not afraid to tell it like it is. Of course, you have to be discriminating and weed out the bad from the good.

Poker Sites

Whether you decide to play poker online or for money (I can't advise you either way), there are two sites that I believe stand out above the others:

One is PokerStars.com, which is one of the largest and most established. PokerStars offers a full suite of no-limit Hold'em tournaments. From freerolls to big-prize events, this site has it all. They have their own annual World Poker Tour event in the Bahamas (for which you can qualify online), and they even offer their own big-time tournament every year called the World Championship of Online Poker.

The other one is FullTiltPoker.com, which is not as big as the others but is a well-run site that has a great interface and many unique features. One of the biggest attractions of this site is the great number of top professionals who play here. These players will play a lot of low entry tournaments and are always willing to talk via the chat feature. In addition, you will receive frequent e-mails from the top pros offering their strategies on specific topics.

About the Author

David Apostolico has been playing poker for over twenty-five years. He has won tournaments in Las Vegas, Atlantic City, and online and has finished in the money at the U.S. Poker Championships. David plays poker on every level from home games to top tournaments with the best professionals in the world including events on the Professional Poker Tour. David is the author of *Tournament Poker and The Art of War, Machiavellian Poker Strategy,* and *Lessons from the Pro Poker Tour.*

David's previous books *Tournament Poker and The Art of War* and *Machiavellian Poker Strategy* help poker players develop the proper attitude and mindset to be successful at the poker table. *Tournament Poker and The Art of War* incorporates the time-honored philosophies contained in Sun Tzu's classic *The Art of War* and applies them to poker tournaments. To be successful in today's highly competitive tournaments, players need the heart of a warrior and the mind of a general. *Machiavellian Poker Strategy* teaches the reader how to shed his everyday self and adopt a new persona when he enters the poker room. With this newfound persona, players will learn how to employ Machiavellian tactics to rule the table like a Prince.

Lessons from the Pro Poker Tour offers critical hand analysis of key poker hands played on the Professional Poker Tour, which is the first invitation-only poker tour designed to attract the world's top players. Most of the hands discussed in that book come from David's personal experience playing on the Professional Poker Tour.

David also writes a regular column for *Card Player* and his blog can be found at holdemradio.com.

David received his J.D., with honors, from the University of North Carolina School of Law in 1988. Upon graduation, David went to work for the

Wall Street law firm of Winthrop, Stimson, Putnam & Roberts where he spent a number of years specializing in mergers and acquisitions. During his legal career, David has found the principles he has learned at the poker table to be enormously useful in his negotiations on behalf of clients large and small from multibillion dollar corporations to family businesses.

David lives with his wife and hree sons outside of Philadelphia where he practices corporate law and plays competitive poker whenever he gets the opportunity.